TAKE
COMMAND

CONTENTS

To all the dozens of men from Second Battalion,
Seventh Marines, who gave life and limb in Al Anbar
Province, Iraq, in 2007 and Helmand Province,
Afghanistan, in 2008; and to the tens of thousands
of men and women in Team Rubicon who refuse to
let service to their country diminish when they
take off their uniform.

Together, your spirit of service and sacrifice can—and
will—change the direction of our entire generation.

CROWN BUSINESS is a trademark and CROWN and the Rising Sun
colophon are registered trademarks of Random House LLC.

Crown Business books are available at special discounts for bulk pur-
chases for sales promotions or corporate use. Special editions, including
personalized covers, excerpts of existing books, or books with corporate
logos, can be created in large quantities for special needs. For more
information, contact Premium Sales at (212) 572-2232 or e-mail
specialmarkets@randomhouse.com.

Library of Congress Cataloging-in-Publication Data
Wood, Jake.
Take command: lessons in leadership: how to be a first responder in
business / Jake Wood.
1. Leadership. 2. Risk. I. Title.
HD57.7.W657 2014
658.4'092—dc23   2014001258

ISBN 978-0-8041-3838-3
eBook ISBN 978-0-8041-3839-0

Printed in the United States of America

Jacket design by Jessie Sayward Bright

10 9 8 7 6 5 4 3 2 1

First Edition

TAKE
COMMAND

Lessons in Leadership:

HOW TO BE

A FIRST RESPONDER

IN BUSINESS

JAKE WOOD

CROWN
BUSINESS

CROWN BUSINESS

New York

TAKE COMMAND

Of every one hundred men in battle, ten should not even be there. Eighty are nothing more than sheep. Nine are the real fighters, we are lucky to have them since they make the battle. Ah, but the one—one is the Warrior—and he brings the others home.

—HERACLITUS, APPROXIMATELY 500 BC

This book is about how to be that one of the hundred, whether on the literal battlefield or the figurative battlefield of business. It's about how to prepare yourself to fight in the face of extreme pressure and uncertainty. How to find and lead the nine who make the battle. And, ultimately, how to bring them all home, victorious. We can't all be warriors, but we can all be leaders— no matter our function—in today's high-stakes world of business.

INTRODUCTION

February 18, 2007

My eyes stinging with sweat, my gaze flittered back and forth between the still-blazing Humvee and the men standing around me. For a moment, I didn't know what to do. Moments earlier I had just been a Marine lance corporal, only slightly higher ranking than a private, riding in the vehicle commander's seat of a Humvee, three trucks back from the front of a vehicle-mounted mission to aid a platoon of Marines stuck in the mud in a dangerous area outside of Fallujah, Iraq. Now, two weeks into my first combat deployment, I was kneeling over the dead body of a friend, Lance Corporal Blake Howey, unsure of what the next move was.

When the first truck had struck the roadside bomb, I'd thought it was just a blown engine. The brief flash of light didn't register and my body couldn't quite feel the concussive blast of the explosion through the thick steel armor of my vehicle. It wasn't long, however, before the chaos consumed us. I'd grabbed my rifle and stepped out of my Humvee, and as I sprinted forward toward the now burning vehicle, I passed my squad leader, Sergeant Rosenberger.

Sergeant Rosenberger had been in the truck that was hit, and his leg was bleeding from a massive piece of shrapnel as a result. Calm, cool, and collected, Sergeant Rosenberger asked me for a radio.

"Rose, you're hit!" I'd exclaimed, looking at his leg.

"Wood, just get me a friggin' radio," he'd replied, attempting not to put any weight on his bloodied limb. I'd pointed Sergeant Rosenberger toward my truck and explained that we had a PRC-119 radio up and running next to the seat I had just left, and with that, Rosenberger stomped away. Moments later I would run across a burning bridge toward the blazing Humvee, dodging pools of burning fuel along the way.

That's how I found myself kneeling in a puddle of blood over the body of a deceased friend, dragged there moments earlier by two other wounded and dazed Marines. By this time Doc Campanali was by Howey's side, gingerly checking for signs of life. Soon after, Corporal Williams came across the bridge from the second truck, just as it became entirely engulfed in raging flames. We were now cut off from the rest of our squad, alone.

Suddenly, my instincts kicked in. We were vulnerable. We were cut off. We had no radios, and a wide canal separated us from the rest of the unit. Looking around, I saw a situation that desperately needed leadership, yet no one was taking charge. Sensing the void left by Sergeant Rosenberger, I stood up. "Hey, Payne, grab security down that way, watch for a follow-on attack," I said, pointing down the road we'd been on. "Latcher, move thirty feet that way and protect the flank." I looked at Corporal Williams, technically the highest-ranking Marine on site, and saw uncertainty. I saw hesitation. This was his second deployment and he outranked me, yet I sensed that he wasn't prepared to lead, right at that critical moment when we needed a leader in the worst way. That's when I knew I had to Take Command.

In 2005 I had just completed four years at the University of Wisconsin, where I'd watched two wars unfold from the comfort of my living room. While tens of thousands of young men and women my age were off fighting and dying in places with names like Najaf and Korengal, I was playing football games in places like Iowa City and Happy Valley. As the Battle of Fallujah raged live on CNN and Fox News, I specifically remember seeing men who looked just like me covered in dirt, grime, and blood as they moved their ragged squads from house to house, fighting entrenched insurgents around every corner. *Leadership,* I thought to myself, *must be at a premium over there.* I'd always thought of myself as a leader. So a few short months after graduation I raised my right hand, swore an oath, and enlisted into the Marine Corps infantry.

During my time on the Wisconsin Badgers football team, I thought I'd cut my teeth when it came to leadership (despite ending up a fairly average football player). I worked hard and did things the right way, and although nobody was looking to me when games were on the line, I was nonetheless looked to for guidance at other times, both on and off the field. And I no doubt learned some incredible leadership lessons playing football for the demanding Barry Alvarez—some of which you will read in this book—but that moment standing over my friend's mangled, bleeding body on February 18, 2007, changed my perspective on what leadership can and should be. I came to realize that while it might feel like the world is hanging in the balance when there are thirty seconds left in the fourth quarter and your team is down 24–27, I had never truly had it "all on the line." The Marines were my chance to find out if I had what it takes to lead when the stakes truly are high.

That moment—that brief flash of light in front of me—changed the course of my life forever. That night in Iraq simultaneously tested almost every component of my leadership mettle—initiative and judgment, fortitude and bearing, decisiveness and the courage to act, and every other quality necessary for high-stakes leadership—in a way that only combat can. This experience didn't *make* me a leader; nor did it show me that I already knew how to lead. Rather, it revealed to me the type of leader I needed to be.

At thirty years old, I am no longer a warrior and will likely never be one again. Today I am the cofounder and CEO of Team Rubicon, a volunteer nonprofit organization born during a phone call with a fellow Marine, William McNulty, just hours after a devastating earthquake hit Haiti. Only roughly a year after returning from my final combat tour in Afghanistan, I found myself watching the chaos unfold in Port-au-Prince, and, just as I had while watching the Battle of Fallujah rage years earlier, I felt an urge to go, to help, to make a difference.

Over the course of three days, William and I began assembling a team and building a half-baked plan to bring medics and medical supplies to the city. Many people thought we were crazy; and, like most entrepreneurs, we probably were. Time and again William and I were told about all the reasons *not* to go—the danger, the uncertainty, not to mention our lack of experience in disaster response. All those people saw were obstacles; but William and I were only focused on solutions. First and foremost, we needed medics—luckily, my college roommate Jeff and his friend Craig were firefighters and medics in Milwaukee, and signed on to help. The next problem we needed to solve was transportation—the airport in Port-au-Prince was shut down to anything but military transport. Fortunately my future brother-in-law, Ryan, offered to pay for plane tickets to the Dominican Republic; that at least got us halfway there. Finally, our nascent team needed a name. William and I spent a half hour bouncing ideas back and forth, and then, out of a list of potential names that he e-mailed me, my eyes fixed on *Rubicon*, a reference to the river Caesar crossed to march on Rome—leading to a point of no return—and I knew we had it. Our crossing into Haiti was our point of no return; it was our Rubicon.

The next day, Team Rubicon launched. We didn't have a perfect plan, but we had enough of the solution to feel confident in taking the first plunge into the unknown. By the time we crossed the border from the Dominican Republic into Haiti, our team had grown from four to eight—a motley crew of mostly strangers that included military veterans, medics, and a Jesuit brother . . . It was like the start of a bad joke!

I was made the team leader of that initial effort, and every day was a unique challenge. The best map we had was a tattered piece of the *Wall Street Journal* I ripped out on my flight down. But despite this very minimal information, the moment we landed, our team began conducting mobile medical triage clinics throughout the ravaged city. We worked with local drivers and local interpreters, and identified the hardest-hit areas. Once on scene, we had to make swift decisions, like how to maintain security, or how to best manage limited resources in order to maximize impact in limited windows of time.

One community, set on a hillside, had seen the earth beneath its houses give way, sliding every single home, one on top of the next, into a ravine. Someone had managed to climb to the road and tack a sign onto a tree. It said: HELP! 600 TRAPPED. We got down that ravine, a handful of human mules lugging supplies, picking our way through debris. We were the first responders to come to their aid. Incredibly, despite our complete dearth of manpower and equipment, our blatant ignorance about the geography and topography of the region (beyond what we could attain intermittently on our iPhones), and our utter lack of disaster relief experience, our response team somehow managed to reach the neediest areas before relief organizations operating with multibillion-dollar budgets and thousands of volunteers. That was the moment I realized we were onto something; that this ragtag group we'd come to call Team

Rubicon could maybe be the start of something larger, a movement to help serve victims of the world's worst natural disasters—and could involve returning military veterans in something larger than themselves, something more humanizing than war, in the process.

In January 2010, William and I started on that entrepreneurial journey together. We incorporated Team Rubicon, Inc., as a nonprofit organization whose mission is to engage returning Iraq and Afghanistan veterans by rapidly and effectively deploying them into crisis situations to provide immediate aid, in turn providing them with the purpose, community, and sense of self they lose when they take off the uniform. We immediately set to work. Like most intrepid entrepreneurs, we didn't know what we had coming, but fear of the unknown never stopped us. From the very beginning we knew our number one priority was to build a first-rate team—a team foolish enough to think it could change the world and smart enough to have a chance. From the beginning we've evaluated each new member of that team based on two questions: Would that person have followed us to Haiti? And, conversely, would we have followed that same person ourselves? The team itself has changed with time, but what hasn't changed is that each person who has committed to this organization, whether as an employee or a volunteer, has inspired us and made us better leaders because they've continued to challenge us. Team Rubicon is theirs as much as it is ours, and they treat it as such. That's the type of team you want when your back is against the wall.

It's true that most of us won't ever be asked to lead a

squad or fire team across an open field under withering enemy fire, or to dig people out of the rubble of a devastating earthquake. It doesn't matter. For that's not what high-stakes leadership is all about. It's about seeing clearly when others are blinded by fear. Building trust by putting yourself on the line before you ask anyone else. Listening to every viewpoint—truly listening—then making the call and owning it. Recognizing the need to take risks—but never foolhardy ones. Making stress work for you, not against you. Realizing that inner strength is not generated by sweet talk or bravado, but by preparation and analysis. Remembering that a leader is only as good as the people who follow her. Understanding that action is often the first step toward a solution.

At this point you might be asking: But what about *me?* You aren't in the infantry, and pray you'll never find yourself a first responder on the ground in an area that's just been hit by a catastrophic tornado, typhoon, flood, or earthquake. Yet I would argue that in today's volatile, high-stakes, fast-paced business climate, we all need to learn to be first responders in our jobs and careers. After all, every profession has its front lines, whether you work on a commodities floor, or in a courtroom, or in a cubicle behind a computer. Sure, the situations aren't exactly the same. But the principles that carry you through to success are. You can become that person who senses the plane is going down and would rather be in the pilot's seat than the passenger's.

This book is about what it takes to be that type of leader. To have clarity of mind and purpose when chaos is all around you. To act when others are paralyzed. To operate at peak performance under risk, and to adapt in the face of the unexpected. To deliver in the clutch. And as my own experience that day outside Fallujah shows, *anyone* can be that type of leader, no matter how much or little experience you have, what your job title is, or how low down you think you are on the totem pole. Whether you're a regional manager or a sales rep or a marketing director or an entrepreneur or [insert any job title here], the ability to jump into that pilot seat and Take Command is the ability to lead and succeed in today's high-stakes, high-pressure business climate. Because in a world where technology is constantly reinventing how we work, global competition is fierce, and industries are being disrupted overnight, success in business requires a new kind of leadership. It requires high-stakes leadership.

You might ask what I know about this special type of leadership. After all, I never made general in the military, or served as the chairman of a Fortune 500 company— I'm not even the type of person we typically think of as commanding the room. But I was a Marine, and if there's one institution guaranteed to teach you how to accept responsibility, how to handle pressure, how to manage fear, how to build a team—how to get the job done—it's the US military. Indeed, they taught me so well that I was invited to join one of the Corps' most elite units—the Marine Scout Sniper Platoon. Furthermore, what I have learned about leadership has continued to evolve with my work at Team Rubicon. There is perhaps no greater leadership challenge than inspiring volunteers to put their lives on the line at a moment's notice—to voluntarily place themselves in disaster-struck areas where the risks range from contaminated water to lack of shelter to rebel and sectarian violence—when they aren't required or beholden to do so. Leading in these kinds of situations has forced me to rethink what it takes to organize, motivate, lead, and inspire in the most stressful and challenging of situations—whether on the battlefield, the disaster zone, or in today's high-stakes world of work. It is those lessons, from building trust to leading with transparency, to managing risk and opportunity, to taking swift, decisive action—making the call and owning it—when everything is on the line, that are found throughout this book.

Still, at times I find myself questioning whether I am qualified to talk about high-stakes leadership, let alone write a book about it. In reality, I view my thoughts on leadership less as an answer and more as an ongoing journey. I am not a great leader, I'm an evolving leader. I'm a leader who has had the privilege of learning invaluable lessons, both from those I've followed and from those I've led. I've been challenged every step along the way by my family, my friends, and my peers. I've been told I need to be better more often than I've been told that I'm "there": wherever "there" is. And, as a young man, I have had both the good and bad fortune of being thrust into some of the toughest leadership positions imaginable. This leadership journey that I'm on continues today, and will continue for the duration of my life. If this book didn't have a deadline, I'd be adding chapters and making edits in perpetuity. It is a testament to this journey that Team Rubicon is no longer the ragtag group of volunteers that found its way to Haiti; that today Team Rubicon boasts over two dozen full-time and scores of part-time staff, and nearly twenty thousand volunteer veterans and first responders. It conducts missions in places ranging from South Sudan to Burma, and from Missouri to New York—over fifty missions by the close of 2013, on four continents. We've responded to tornadoes and typhoons, hurricanes and refugee crises, and tons of other disasters in between. We have made speed, efficiency, and impact the hallmarks of our operations. Our ability to move quickly, nimbly, and yet decisively is central to achieving our goal to do more with less.

We aim to help out where others fear to go or cannot reach. If you ask me why the men and women who put their lives on the line to help victims of natural disasters do what they do—for no reward other than what they feel inside—it's because when we ask them to risk their lives to help others, they know we have done our part to define the mission, assess the situation, and calculate the risks. People don't want their time or talents wasted. They have a low tolerance for bullshit, and for excuses—and so should you. People follow leaders who will stand with them, not pronounce from the top floor or issue orders from HQ. Ultimately, if you give them the chance, and a reason, to trust you, it is utterly astounding what those asked to serve will do.

I enlisted in the Marines first and foremost to serve. But I also went to learn. I thought I wanted to learn how to become a man, but over time I realized what I needed to learn was how to become a better leader. The military came through for me. It taught me the mindset of the guy who steps forward and says he'll Take Command; who, when everything matters, when it's really life or death, coolly assesses—the situation, the risks, the character of his team—then gets down to the business of getting everyone through the battle.

But what I didn't know until after I left the Marines was how valuable the leadership skills I learned there would be *off* the battlefield. That there's as strong a need for stand-up leaders outside a war zone as there is inside. How they could help me help others not just through Team Rubicon, but in every aspect of life. Today we all live in uncertain times, and we're all searching for firm ground. We all want to be the people who remain steady even as others lose their footing. And while no one can see into the future, it doesn't take a crystal ball to know that one day, most of us will be confronted with a situation in which the stakes are high, the risks considerable, and the options not ideal. It might be a key business decision we have avoided making. Or a mistake we made in the past and don't want to face. Perhaps we have to meet face-to-face with angry investors wanting quick answers to tough questions. Or maybe it's a project that has to be completely redone at the eleventh hour, an unsettling merger or reorganization, or a surprise competitor who emerged out of nowhere. This book is about how to respond to these everyday business challenges with the speed, agility, and bias toward action of a first responder. Because whatever your particular chal-lenge is, when the pressure is on and the stakes are high, those same leadership skills and principles critical to mission success in the disaster zone or on the battlefield are equally critical to our professional survival.

This book will show you how to apply those lessons to not only survive but *thrive* in high-stakes situations—business or otherwise. It's meant not so much as a step-by-step play-book, but rather as a tool kit to help you lead and succeed at those clutch moments when the pressure and the risks—as well as the opportunities—are at their highest. It's a set of principles showing you, among other things, how to spot and hit priority targets, how to gather the best and most useful intelligence, how to make decisions and craft plans even in the absence of complete information, and then how to execute those plans decisively—while still being nimble and adaptable enough to iterate on a dime as the terrain changes. It's about how to manage risk, operate at peak performance under stress, and adapt swiftly and decisively to the unexpected. And, perhaps most important, it's about how to build teams with the highest impact, and then inspire those teams to follow you into battle. It's meant as a guide to the how, when, and why of resolute, lead-from-the-front leadership, a set of principles that make sense in all kinds of situations.

By writing this book, I hope to make what I've learned from my experiences in the military and running an organization like Team Rubicon available to all kinds of people at every level; to help everyone from middle managers to members of the board apply these principles from the disaster zone and the battlefield in order to become a first responder in their career or organization. At its core, high-stakes leadership can be summarized by four simple steps:

prepare, analyze, decide, then just do it. Find the best of yourself and your team in the worst circumstances. Hit top form when the pressure is highest. Feel calmest when the stress is most enormous.

Take Command.

PREPARE

Victorious warriors win first and then go to war,
while defeated warriors go to war first
and then seek to win.
—SUN TZU

Thousands of years ago Sun Tzu, perhaps the most
famous military philosopher of all time, wrote this time-
less maxim; and throughout history leaders have proven it
true—through both victory and defeat. Preparation—
of yourself, of your team, and of your organizational
culture—is critical for success in high-stakes situations,
business and otherwise. Don't be the leader caught un-
prepared when everything is on the line and it's too late.
Instead, be the leader who strides calmly and confidently
toward uncertainty, with the knowledge that no one is
better prepared to face whatever challenges might come
his way.

No matter what your job responsibilities are or how

many people you lead, you *can* be better prepared for the business challenges that lie ahead. The first step is to reflect on what you're currently doing, and what you can be doing better. Are you challenging yourself and building a level of personal fortitude capable of overcoming the trials you expect to face? Look around at your team members. Are they capable and motivated to achieve the highest impact; to operate at peak performance when the pressure is mounting and a lot is on the line? Is your team or organization built on a culture of trust, transparency, and accountability so that people are inspired to follow you into the line of fire when the stakes are at their highest?

If the answer to each of these questions is not a resounding "Yes," then preparation starts now.

LESSON 1

Preparation: Lessons from the Marines' Most Elite School

"Gentlemen, let me start by telling you the next ten weeks of your life will be the most miserable stretch of your pitiful existence," the instructor bellowed as he paced back and forth across the cement. My muscles, exhausted from holding my body in the push-up position for what seemed like hours, screamed at me to give up. Through the tops of my eyes I could barely make out the tan, dusty boots of the other instructors, lined up in front of the hut that contained the schoolhouse. "This is the most difficult training that the Marine Corps offers, and it is the finest sniper school in the world. You have worked for years to earn a slot in this course, and over the next two and a half months, we're going to learn which of you are truly prepared for the pain we're about to level on you."

I stole glances to my left and right, quickly assessing which of the thirty-two Marines would still be around on graduation day. I was fresh off my first combat tour in Iraq, where I had helped lead a squad of thirteen men on nearly two hundred combat patrols. At the end of that tour I had been approached by the chief scout in the Sniper Platoon, and was asked to try out. Having worked with some of the sniper teams during my tour, I knew that they were the best Marines in the battalion. After a grueling weeklong selection process, I had been accepted into the unit along with about eight others, and we immediately began preparation for Sniper School—pushing ourselves to our physical limits, beginning and ending every day with written tests, and honing the technical skills that make Marine snipers the modern battlefield's most lethal weapon.

Four months later I found myself hovering over a pool of my own sweat, attempting to determine whether I had in fact prepared enough. Of the thirty-two Marines beginning this class with me, every single one of them was the absolute best their platoon had, and many of them hailed from Recon and Special Operations. They were decorated combat veterans with multiple tours, many of them back for their second attempt to pass. Statistics said that over half of us would not graduate, and at that moment I thought I would be in the wrong half.

The instructor stopped pacing and turned to face us. His voice lowered, almost softened, and he said, "We are going to push you to your absolute limits. We are going to test your physical, mental, and emotional stamina in ways you can't possibly imagine. We're going to take away your food, your sleep, and probably your sanity. We will make you calculate wind formulas until your mind spins, and do our best to turn you on one another. Everything we do will be a test, and the moment you fail to meet the standard, you're gone. There is no room for error. There is no quitting. The SEALs have their cute little bell that you can ring to quit; that's them. If you try to quit here you will be nonjudicially punished for failure to follow orders. Men, I can only promise you one thing—that if you have the honor of graduating from this school you will be ready; ready to hunt men on the battlefield."

He was not lying. Sniper School was the hardest experience of my life. But, hellish as it was, it sure taught me how to prepare myself physically, mentally, and emotionally for the tough combat situations I found in the barren wastelands of Afghanistan. Throughout that seven-month tour, I came up against countless seemingly insurmountable challenges—from shortages of water to fierce firefights to gut-wrenching dysentery—but not one of those moments caught me without the appropriate mental, emotional, and physical tools to succeed.

Marine Sniper School has nearly a 70 percent failure rate, which is even more significant because candidates are so thoroughly screened to attend in the first place. Many people would falsely assume that the majority of people fail because of a lack of technical skills, like poor marksmanship. In fact, they could not be further from the truth. Being a Marine sniper isn't just about hitting enemy targets—in other words, shooting people. To the contrary, a Marine scout-sniper's primary mission is far more complex than that—it's to go deep within enemy territory to collect and accurately relay information to generate battlefield intelligence. Their *secondary* mission—to provide precision fire on selected targets—is about sheer marksmanship. But to accomplish the former requires tremendous cognitive forbearance, including, among other things, a tolerance for risk and uncertainty, the ability to operate effectively under pressure, and a knack for analyzing only the facts—without conjecture or emotion. In other words, the same skills it takes to lead and succeed in today's fast-paced, high-stakes, volatile world of business.

It is because of these requirements, therefore, that Sniper School tests the boundaries of human endurance. How will the Marines in the class interact on only three hours of sleep? Will a lack of food affect their ability to demonstrate sound judgment? What is their breaking point? To test these limits, instructors push students every day through a series of carefully designed exercises that constantly challenge them physically, mentally, and emotionally.

Of course, most of us don't have jobs that demand us to function on three hours of sleep, or hike for miles in the desert without any food, or hit enemy targets hundreds of yards out in the bed of a moving vehicle. Yet anyone who expects or hopes to achieve consistent success in the business world today—a world where the hours are often grueling, the challenges are ever-increasing, the uncertainties are rapidly growing, and the competition is increasingly fierce—must prepare for situations that require mental, physical, and emotional toughness, be it a major proposal that must be scrapped and completely redone at the last minute, a forced relocation to an undesirable and far-flung corner of the globe, an abusive new boss who denigrates you at every turn, or a downsizing that forces you to work on an austerity budget while cash flow is tight. These situations, and countless others like them, require you to be physically, mentally, and emotionally prepared, whether it's to work for fifty-two straight hours, fight the alienation and loneliness of a city where you have no friends or family or trappings of home, turn your boss's verbal abuse into the fuel that motivates and energizes you, or choke down ramen noodles for the tenth night in a row. The point is that no matter what business or career you're in, and no matter what your particular challenges might be, the better prepared you are to face unexpected turbulence, the better you'll be able to lead and succeed in those situations where the pressure is highest, the stress is fiercest, and the risks—as well as the rewards—are greatest.

PILLARS OF PREPARATION

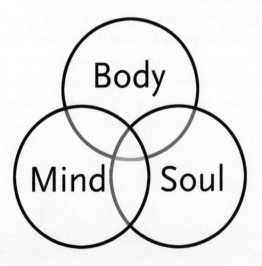

In preparing ourselves for any business challenge that might come our way, it's important to note that all three areas—mind, body, and soul—should be equally addressed. Why? Because in business and life, just as in the Marines, the three are interconnected and interdependent; weakness in any one single area will ultimately lead to a breakdown in another. How? It's really quite simple. Physical weakness can often lead to a lack of confidence; a lack of confidence leads to indecisive leadership or decision making; poor decision making leads to failure. A weak mind allows the body's pain to trump the mind's will to continue on, ultimately leading to physical defeat. Finally, emotional weakness eats away at the mind's ability to think clearly, clouding judgment and decision making. These are just simple examples, and many more abound. And while the business world may not require quite the same *level* of preparedness as entering a disaster zone after a hurricane or picking off enemy insurgents in the Iraqi deserts, I've found that many of the techniques I learned for improving my physical, mental, and emotional preparedness—both in the Marines and, later on, on the front lines of disaster relief missions to areas decimated by floods, tornadoes, and earthquakes—apply equally to today's high-pressure, high-stress, fast-paced business climate.

Preparing the Body

Preparing the body is perhaps the least obvious pillar when it comes to business, yet physical preparation plays a critical role in increasing one's ability to overcome any type of challenge. Fitness, at its core, is about health; and good health, at the end of the day, allows us to perform at our best. Challenging ourselves physically not only gives us physical stamina, it increases our mental capacity and releases healthy endorphins that make us feel better—making the second and third pillars, our mind and spirit, even easier to prepare.

Naturally, physical preparation was a critical component of my job in the Marines. Perhaps just as obvious, physical preparation and fitness are key factors in the success of my work with Team Rubicon—but not only for the reasons you might imagine. Certainly, while responding to disasters I have found myself in a multitude of situations where physical performance could mean life or death. One such example happened on the first day of our first mission to Port-au-Prince, Haiti, when responding to the deadly earthquake there. We had hired a local driver to take us all the way across the city to a displaced persons' camp, where we set up a triage clinic and, over the course of a single day, treated hundreds of critically wounded patients. But as the day drew to a close and we saw the sun begin to inch toward the horizon, we began to get nervous that our driver had forgotten to pick us up. As the hours ticked by and the driver failed to materialize, our fears were realized, and we faced a critical decision—begin hiking over twelve kilometers back to our base of operations across tricky terrain, at night, in a city on the brink of anarchy; or bed down in the displaced persons' camp and risk being attacked and possibly killed for our supplies. My gut reaction was to hike out, but, as I looked around at the team members, I realized that not all of us were physically prepared to make the journey, and we were immediately reduced to the one, potentially more dangerous option. (Fortunately, we were able to flag down a local driver and pay him $200 cash to take us back, but please note that you can't always buy your way out of a lack of preparation!)

The less obvious manner in which physical fitness is critical to our work at Team Rubicon has less to do with feats of strength or forced marches across potentially hostile cities, and more to do with the simple stamina needed to operate at a high mental capacity for prolonged periods of time on limited sleep. In late 2012, a massive super-storm made landfall on the Eastern seaboard of the United States. Hurricane Sandy, as it was called, wreaked havoc across New Jersey and New York, shutting down huge swaths of major metropolitan areas, and completely overwhelming emergency response authorities. Team Rubicon, which had been pre-positioned since twenty-four hours before the storm, immediately sprang into action.

Watching the devastation unfold on television and reading the reports coming in from our team leaders in the field, we made the decision to relocate our entire headquarters element from Los Angeles to Brooklyn in order to better manage our response efforts. Once on the ground, our headquarters team set up a temporary office on New York City's Roosevelt Island and set out to manage all aspects of the response, from coordinating the efforts of all the various agencies that wanted to pitch in; to the logistics of flying in 150 team leaders from over 35 states; to feeding, housing, and showering more than 350 volunteers in a city that had zero hotel vacancies due to the storm. For ten straight days, this team of a dozen ate and worked in the same single-room office until the wee hours of morning, when they would attempt to catch a few hours of sleep under their makeshift desks before starting all over.

Though our efforts that week were conducted in an office, instead of on the front lines, and were comprised mainly of unglamorous administrative work, rather than dropping out of helicopters and digging people out of rubble, they were no less strenuous, and our success hinged no less on our physical training, our experience in pushing our bodies to their limits. You see, the human body is remarkably malleable, and pushing it in one manner—dead-lifting heavy weights, or perhaps running a marathon—prepares it (and your mind) for all other physical challenges, whether it's making hard decisions at a moment's notice, mobilizing diverse and far-flung teams into action, or coordinating a massive relief effort—all while operating on little food and sleep. It should be no wonder that many former college and professional athletes move on from their athletic careers and have tremendous success in the business world. Sure, they have a good place to start—access to capital, a personal brand—but those things only create opportunity. It's their ability—learned on the field and in the gym—to function better under pressure, push themselves harder and longer, and operate at peak performance under less than ideal conditions that makes them so successful in the high-octane world of business.

What does this mean for you? You might be thinking that, short of a career change that includes hunting the

Taliban or responding to massive earthquakes, physical preparation can take a backseat to all of life's other priorities. You couldn't be more wrong. There is no easier way to improve discipline, build character, and push limits than through physical training. No matter what level of fitness you can currently claim, you have the opportunity to make yourself more resilient, more reliable, and more confident with physical preparation.

What's the first step? Set a goal with a long time-horizon. It is critical that this goal be both meaningful and measurable. This could mean completing a marathon, losing twenty-five pounds, or being able to do twenty pull-ups. A bad goal would be ambiguous—to "get in shape," for example. Vague goals allow you to fudge your standard of success, which allows you to justify less effort, which ultimately leads you to fail.

If your goal is intimidating, try breaking it into smaller, more manageable chunks. A marathon, for example, is 26.2 miles, which might as well be a thousand for some. But at its simplest, a marathon is a series of twenty-six one-mile races, and a single mile should intimidate no one.

Next, establish a program, and teach yourself the discipline to stick with it. Discipline and accountability will be discussed in depth later in the book, but the important takeaway is this: No excuses! Nobody likes hearing their alarm clock go off at 6:00 a.m. on Monday morning. It doesn't matter; get up and run the six miles you have penciled in on your calendar. The mental clarity you'll enjoy for the rest of the day will be worth the effort.

Finally, test your limits. At some point, with diligence

and effort, you will meet your goal. What do you do then? You set a new, preferably unrelated, one. If you just ran a marathon, now challenge yourself to double your maximum weight on the back-squat. If you just lost twenty-five pounds, challenge yourself to add half of it back on in muscle. Pretty soon the cycle of challenge-progress-goal-challenge will provide you with the confidence to take on anything that life hands you—be it a new job, an impossible case, or a pesky coworker. You will be able to take challenges as they come and throw them into the same cycle: Acknowledge and accept the challenge, make and measure progress against it through diligence and maximal effort, and finally conquer it.

Yes, pushing your physical limits can be hard, but as I learned in the Marines, *pain is temporary*. The joy of victory quickly washes away the temporary pain felt along the journey.

Preparing the Mind

Mental toughness (born in part through physical preparation), acuity, and sound judgment are equally critical to leading effectively in today's high-pressure business environment. In the Marines, dangerous conditions test your ability to focus intently, complicated weapons systems require ever-increasing mental calculations, and vague rules of engagement constantly force you to make high-stakes decisions under stress—all critical skills in today's world of business. The battlefield is the last place you want to discover that you don't have what it takes mentally to stay strong when the going gets tough. So how did the instructors prepare our minds in Sniper School? They built mental challenges into every single physical activity. For example, a typical day would begin with physical training, where they might have us bear-crawl backward up a mountain and then sprint back down, only to find a written test at the bottom. Then the real tests of our fortitude would begin.

Sometimes, our chief instructor would give us a memory game, where they would reveal a set of ten random items on display—a pen, watch, and newspaper clipping, for example—for only a period of about fifteen seconds. Then, later in the day, or even week, typically after a particularly strenuous moment, they would announce it was time for the memory test, and everyone would drop what they were doing, pull out a piece of paper, and try to re-create all ten objects. A student would have sixty seconds to write down the name, color, size, condition, shape, and defining characteristic of all ten items—no easy task, especially when you're exhausted from having just run five miles in the desert.

At the time these seemed to be nothing more than maddeningly impossible games (or the cruel machinations of heartless platoon leaders, as it sometimes felt), but later I realized how much they improved my ability to execute difficult mental tasks in all kinds of situations.

You can create challenges like these for yourself; some of the sharpest people I have met since leaving the Marines practice their own "civilian" versions of these mental exercises. While waiting for a plane to take off they are completing a sudoku puzzle under a self-imposed time constraint rather than reading a gossip magazine, or doing a cross-word instead of watching TV, or reading a book (hopefully this one) that expands their horizons rather than play-ing Angry Birds on their phone. The embodiment of this type of person was my chief scout in the Sniper Platoon, Shawn Beidler. On our deployment to Afghanistan, Shawn brought only a small handful of personal items, yet among them were his college Calculus II and Organic Chemistry books, and a Rubik's Cube. When asked why, he would re-spond with something like, "I learned it once; why would I let my brain atrophy?"

The point is that our brain is perhaps the most pow-erful muscle we have, and if we want to operate at peak performance—whether in the classroom, the boardroom, or the line of fire—we need to keep it constantly active. So create little memory tests or mental challenges for your-self throughout the day. Do sudoku or other puzzles, even silly word games like seeing how many anagrams you can create out of a person's name. The better shape that men-tal muscle is in, the better prepared you'll be to solve the myriad problems and issues that inevitably come at you in rapid fire over the course of a hectic workday.

But keeping your brain strong isn't the only way to im-prove your mental preparedness for all the unexpected obstacles you'll have to navigate, difficult people you'll have to deal with, and tough decisions you'll have to make (often with incomplete or incorrect information) in your professional life. At Team Rubicon, when we go on a relief mission we never know quite what to expect when we get there. Will the terrain be navigable? Will the authorities be welcoming? What will the medical priorities be? To be mentally prepared for these unknowns, we employ two very different yet equally important strategies: We amass as much knowledge about the region and the disaster as possible, and we draw on the power of positive thinking. These skills are equally important in business.

Knowledge preparation involves identifying needs and gaps in what is known, and subsequently taking steps to fill them; it is essentially building the mental tool kit needed to solve problems. Positive thinking is the deliberate visualization and mental rehearsal of positive outcomes. Both are critical to being successful in high-stakes situations both in the disaster zone and in the workplace.

KNOWLEDGE

Before discussing how to arm yourself with the knowledge required to solve problems, make quick decisions, and put out metaphorical fires at work, we should clear one thing up. As Albert Einstein, one of the most brilliant men of the last three centuries, once quipped, "Information is not knowledge." While short on words, this quote is long on wisdom. There is a critical difference between information and knowledge, and understanding that distinction will impact how you go about preparing your mind.

At its simplest, information is the "what," while knowledge is the "why." Information contains clearly demonstrated, indisputable facts and anecdotes, and is critical in any decision-making process. Knowledge, however, is the understanding of why or how information came to be.

The point is that only the why is what will allow you

to manipulate that knowledge into a functional framework for effective decision making. Let's look at an example. When the United States went to war in Afghanistan in 2001, they did so knowing that Afghanistan was a graveyard for armies of some of the world's greatest empires. The Greeks, the British, and the Russians are just a few examples of the mighty militaries that have fallen victim to Afghanistan's unique terrain, fierce people, and deeply tribal culture. Much has been written about these failed military campaigns, which is why, in the lead-up to the invasions of both Afghanistan and Iraq, Marine General James Mattis, a legendary leader known for his voracious reading, issued a required reading list for his commanders. According to lore (there are more legends circulating about Mattis than can be counted), a junior officer e-mailed him, complaining about the volume of reading and questioning its value in light of all the other tactical and technical combat training that was needed.

Reportedly, Mattis replied with a long and eloquent e-mail in which he explained the following:

> Thanks to my reading, I have never been caught flat-footed by any situation, never at a loss for how any problem has been addressed (successfully or unsuccessfully) before. It doesn't give me all the answers, but it lights what is often a dark path ahead. . . . Ultimately, a real understanding of history means that we face NOTHING new under the sun.
>
> For all the "4th Generation of War" intellectuals running around today saying that the nature of war

has fundamentally changed, the tactics are wholly new, etc., I must respectfully say . . . "Not really": Alex the Great would not be in the least bit perplexed by the enemy that we face right now in Iraq, and our leaders going into this fight do their troops a disservice by not studying (studying, vice just reading) the men who have gone before us.

We have been fighting on this planet for 5,000 years and we should take advantage of their experience. "Winging it" and filling body bags as we sort out what works reminds us of the moral dictates and the cost of incompetence in our profession. As commanders and staff officers, we are coaches and sentries for our units: How can we coach anything if we don't know a hell of a lot more than just the [tactics, techniques, and procedures]? What happens when you're on a dynamic battlefield and things are changing faster than higher [Headquarters] can stay abreast? Do you not adapt because you cannot conceptualize faster than the enemy's adaptation? . . . And how can you be a sentinel and not have your unit caught flat-footed if you don't know what the warning signs are—that your unit's preps are not sufficient for the specifics of a tasking that you have not anticipated?

What Mattis is trying to say is that leaders have a near-moral imperative to dive deeper beyond the what and get to the why. The infantry tactics, techniques, and procedures are simply the "whats" of war-fighting—applying them effectively, in a manner that keeps your men safe and destroys the enemy with limited collateral damage, is knowledge. It is a deeper understanding of how they have been applied in the past, creating a framework in your mind that prepares you for future scenarios.

Whether on the battlefield, in the disaster zone, or at the workplace, there are three general categories of knowledge:

- Things you know you know
- Things you know you don't know
- Things you don't know you don't know (ignorance)

The first two are tangible, and one can think of them in terms of the actual things that are known. For example, I know how an internal combustion engine works. I also know that I don't know how a jet engine works—but if I decide that this would be important knowledge for me to have, I can simply go out and learn. The third, however, is an abstract list. While intangible, ignorance is just as real. The first step is to accept that we are all ignorant to some degree—the bigger challenge is to then reduce that ignorance.

How do we reduce ignorance? Since by definition we can't reliably pinpoint our areas of ignorance, the key is to expose ourselves to a wide variety of experiences and devour information across different sources. Find a way to force news into your life, whether by reading a newspaper over breakfast, listening to satellite radio on your commute, or setting aside thirty minutes during the workday to peruse reputable blogs. Be sure to read across a wide variety of topics, from all different points of view, and avoid paying attention only to news related to your profession or interests. Another great way to expose yourself to knowledge is to travel; and don't stay at the Four Seasons.

In your work life, get out on the front lines of your business, whether by visiting the factory floor or fulfillment center, spending a few weeks shadowing someone in a different department, attending a conference or seminar that doesn't apply directly to everyday duties—anything that shifts your perspective to that of those you lead (we'll discuss this more later). In fact, the farther you stray from your comfort zone, the more likely you are to encounter and absorb knowledge you didn't know you didn't know.

POSITIVE THINKING AND VISUALIZATION

The second component of mental preparation is positive thinking. Now, you might be thinking, "If I wanted to learn about positive thinking, I would have bought a Tony Robbins book!" Unfortunately, positive thinking is often associated with touchy-feely personalities and is dismissed as an unserious tool for achieving success. People who take this stance are missing out on a tremendous technique that improves a leader's confidence and increases his ability to act quickly and decisively in high-pressure situations.

I have used positive thinking, specifically visualization, throughout my life—regardless of activity. I'm pretty sure it began with football, where as a play was called in the huddle I would mentally visualize my portion of execution: coming off the snap hard; making contact with the defensive player; getting the proper fit and using the right technique; driving hard through my legs and hips; and finally, finishing through the whistle. Sometimes it worked like I visualized, other times it didn't (one can assume it failed as often as it worked, considering my sputtered college football career!), but I have no doubt that it made me a better player.

While practicing marksmanship in the Sniper Platoon I would use the same technique, "nailing" every shot a dozen times in my mind before ever pulling the trigger. I would rehearse mentally the steps and checks needed to fire accurately: relax the body; melt down onto the gun; check my cheek weld; control my breathing; observe the target; slow, steady trigger squeeze.

I still use positive thinking and visualization today in my role as one of the public faces of Team Rubicon, particularly when I speak in front of crowds. In this case, I imagine what I want the audience to walk away with, whether it is a feeling, a piece of information, or an impetus to act. I then visualize what this end-state, this goal, looks like. It might be nodding heads and murmurs, or perhaps even boisterous clapping; regardless, I visualize that objective and use it as a goal that I steer the talk toward.

Positive thinking and visualization are critical exercises for anyone who has to perform, and who will have that performance judged in any business context. This could be a courtroom lawyer who wants to make his closing argument a slam dunk, or an early-stage entrepreneur who is pitching to venture capitalists for financing, or an account manager trying to nail that key client or customer. In any of these cases, and in many others, visualizing success and thinking positively about your own ability to achieve it gives you the confidence and mental acuity to make those outcomes a reality.

Preparing the Soul

In the Marines, the instructors would frequently test not just our physical stamina but also our emotional wherewithal. The circumstances always changed, but the tools— the withholding of food and sleep—rarely did. It was not uncommon for the instructors to dangle a promise of hot chow in front of us, only to rip it away at the last possible moment. Or, after a long two-day exercise, reward only the team that finished last with the opportunity to sleep, while sending the "winners" back out to repeat the exercise, breeding contempt among peers. It sounds cruel, but learning how to check your emotions at the door will make you more even-keeled. Knowing that not everything (including whether your sniper instructors are going to needlessly yank your hot chow) is under your control—and accepting it—makes it easier to accept the brutal reality of whatever circumstance you face. There is a time to lead with emotion, but it is rarely when rational decisions need to be made.

Preparing the soul is a somewhat abstract concept, but essentially it involves making sure you have emotional and spiritual balance. The first step is ensuring that critical relationships in your life—God (or whatever higher power you might subscribe to), family, loved ones, and friends—are in order. The second is finding the positive value that your work brings to those around you—in essence, finding the meaning behind it all.

TAKE CARE OF RELATIONSHIPS, AND THEY WILL TAKE CARE OF YOU

I will not enter into a discussion on religion, as I find the subject too personal for the pages of this book. However, I will say that while it may be tempting, dangerous or high-stakes situations are not the time to reflect on the meaning of life and how it all ends—that's a determination you need to make for yourself well in advance!

Beyond religion, though, there are other ways to achieve preparedness of spirit, and the primary one is through healthy relationships. I have seen time and again strong men (I say "men" primarily because of my experiences in all-male units in the military) break down during critical situations because they have failed to maintain or nurture strong relationships with their families, in particular their spouses. I can't count the number of times, while deployed to Iraq and Afghanistan, I witnessed outstanding Marines become liabilities to their units because of strife at home. These weren't all inevitable situations; many of them could have been avoided had the Marines taken the maintenance of their relationships as seriously as the maintenance of their weapons. Was this *always* the case? Of course not, and it would be irresponsible of me to suggest it. However, it was almost inevitable that when a marriage or relationship would falter or fail, the Marine's performance would falter along with it.

How do you avoid neglecting relationships in the face of the ever-increasing demands our jobs place on our focus, our energy, and our time? To be honest, it is very difficult, especially in today's hypercompetitive 24/7 work environment. For those of us who are driven to succeed, it is often too easy to get sucked into a cycle of work-work-work-sleep-repeat, finding little time to decompress or even eat, let alone carve out time to watch a movie with our loved one, or make it to our child's recital. We rationalize this by telling ourselves it's not the time away that will cause our relationships to fail, but instead it's not succeeding at work that will cause the kinds of problems and stress that breed resentment, anger, and discontent in a family or marriage. But this wrongheaded belief that professional success will lead to our personal happiness ends up sabotaging both our professional performance *and* our personal relationships—inflicting great pain not only on ourselves, but on our loved ones along the way.

	Cause	Effect
Incorrect	Failing at work	Leads to distractions at home and failed relationships.
Correct	Failing at home	Leads to failing at work.

Later in this book I will talk about how we must eliminate or control as many variables as possible in stressful times. Well, relationships are a variable that we *can* control, well in advance of a crisis or high-pressure situation, and in fact we must, in order to approach decisions and tasks with a clear mind. Healthy relationships provide the bedrock on which you can lean—a safe haven to which you can escape or find comfort—when times are difficult. Take care of your loved ones, and they'll take care of you.

FIND THE MEANING

In a world where the boundaries between work and life are becoming increasingly blurred, many people seem to have the mindset that "you are what you do." What does your work make you? What do you want it to make you? Many of us will find ourselves answering those two questions very differently. There are careers, and then there are callings— things you were born to do. Sometimes they are one and the same; other times not. But just because we may not see our career as a calling doesn't mean we should quit our jobs, move to Fiji, and open a surf shop. Instead, we can all do better at finding the hidden value that our work brings to the world. If we find that hidden value—whether we work at a nonprofit, a law firm, an investment bank, or as a small business owner—we will undoubtedly work with more passion and drive higher results.

When William and I were first starting Team Rubicon, for example, we were struggling for money in a bad way. I ended up securing a meeting with a very successful partner at a billion-dollar private equity group in Los Angeles, and prepared for it diligently for weeks, writing a business plan, practicing my pitch, and pressing my best suit. The meeting itself went incredibly well, and the gentleman immediately committed to cutting a $25,000 check. Then he leaned back in his chair and got a little nostalgic. He said to me, "You know what, Jake, what you're doing . . . it's incredible. It has meaning. It brings value. I see that. Me? I try to do what I can. I give more than ten percent of everything I earn here"—he swept his arm around his corner office on the fifteenth floor of a mid-Wilshire high-rise—"to my church and to charity. Two years ago I went to my pastor and told him I wanted to retire so that I could become a youth pastor. Jake, I kid you not, that pastor looked me in the eye and told me I was crazy. He said, 'Bob, the only thing you know you're good at in this world is making money, and you're good at giving it away. You have far more potential as a philanthropist than as a youth pastor.'" Bob then chuckled and continued, "So here I am. Now I just keep making money so I can give it away."

What's the moral of this story? You don't have to work for a nonprofit like Team Rubicon to know you're making a difference in the world. To the naked eye, Bob might seem a greedy capitalist, driven by the desire to increase the vast wealth of his powerful clients. But in reality, Bob continues to fly 100,000 miles a year closing private equity deals so he can continue *to give large sums of money away*. The truth is that everyone has the potential to find meaning in their work, no matter what they do. Entrepreneurs can invent products that change lives—and make them affordable to all. Bankers and lenders can find ways to help new families buy their first home. Lawyers can protect environmental and human rights. Engineers can make our cars and trains and buses safer. Movie directors can bring joy and laughter to lives through the big screen.

Notice I inserted "can" into each of those statements. Doing good—using our talents to make a difference—is a choice. How will you choose to use yours?

FORTITUDE: THE SUM OF THE THREE PILLARS OF PREPARATION

What does a person who has diligently prepared his body, mind, and soul become? The answer is: a person of unquestionable fortitude. It is this trait, fortitude, that defines someone willing to persevere and overcome any circumstance, regardless of odds or stakes or obstacles. Fortitude is that special something that you can't quite put your finger on when talking about the person that just "gets it done."

At Team Rubicon, as in the Sniper Platoon, we look for people with fortitude, because it's not something we can bestow upon them, and it's not anything we can ask them to develop. It's a personal choice, made by the individual, to make themselves more resilient. Successful people develop a high level of fortitude, and the best teams demand it.

Examples of fortitude can be found in every industry, at every level, at any time in history. Fortitude is Abraham Lincoln losing numerous bids for public office, only to become the most celebrated president in our nation's history.

Fortitude is John McCain enduring seven years in a North Vietnamese POW camp despite offers to be let free simply because his father was an admiral in the Navy. Fortitude is Steve Jobs being fired from Apple, the company he founded, only to return years later and turn it into the most successful company in history—while battling cancer. Fortitude is the child that rises up out of the foster system to attend college and start her own business.

Fortitude is the common thread of great, enduring success; and the best part about it is that we can all develop it—if we diligently prepare our minds, bodies, and spirits.

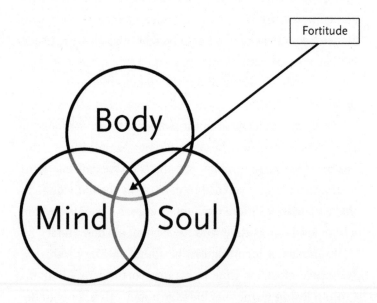

MISSION BRIEF

- Physical, mental, and emotional preparation are interconnected, and equally important for success in life. A weakness in any single area weakens our ability to succeed.
- Physical challenges provide us the opportunity to constantly push ourselves and become accustomed to overcoming obstacles and meeting difficult goals.
- The key to achieving knowledge is to accept that we are all ignorant in some area or another, then work to identify what you don't know, and voraciously address it.
- Focus on the "why" and not the "what."
- Embrace visualization and positive thinking, always focusing on the outcomes you wish to produce.
- If you take care of your relationships, your relationships will take care of you.
- Find meaning in what you do, regardless of title, industry, or function. If you can't find it, find something else to do.
- A fully prepared mind, body, and soul lead to a person of fortitude, willing and able to overcome any obstacle.

LESSON 2

Build a High-Impact Team

"Listen, William, I am hearing what you're saying, and of course the intelligence is concerning—I mean, it's from a credible source; but . . ." I paused, gathering my thoughts. "But I have to admit, I think we have a good team in place— the right team. We have skill, experience, and, most important, the willingness to try."

There was a brief pause on the other end of the line. Finally, William's voice broke the silence. "I agree. It's the right team. Let's do this."

Lowering the phone from my ear, I thumbed the red Off button. William and I had just had a briefly heated conversation about new information that had come his way through a friend in the intelligence community. The picture that was being painted on the ground in Haiti was bad—very bad. Most people we were talking to were advising us not to go. They were warning us about the unstable populace, the lack of clean water, the overwhelmed supply points, and, of course, the diseases like malaria and cholera. Even after thirty-six hours of collecting information about what we were potentially facing, many things remained unclear. About one thing, however, we were certain—we had a good team on our side.

At that time our team was small—only four of us, including William, who had a background in Marine infantry and counterintelligence, and had spent a few years overseas; Jeff Lang, an inner-city firefighter and medic; Craig Parello, a firefighter and former Marine; and me, a former Marine sniper with two combat tours under my belt. Yet somehow this motley crew, which was so resolute in its mission, would inspire four others to join its ranks while en route to Haiti. The first was when William, wearing his Marine Corps BDU pants on the tarmac of the airport in Washington, DC, was approached by a gentleman on the shuttle bus. "You look like you're going to Haiti to do something crazy, Marine," Mark Hayward, a former Army Special Forces medic who eventually became our fifth member, said as he leaned over the aisle. "I'm on my way down there myself, but looking for a crew. May I join?" Meanwhile, on the airplane from Milwaukee to the Dominican Republic, Jeff Lang met a doctor from San Francisco who was flying down and expecting to work at a clinic on the Dominican side of the border. That doctor, Eduardo, became Team Rubicon member number six. Then, while standing at the baggage claim in Santo Domingo, I was approached by a another doctor, in scrubs. "You look like you're going to Haiti, young man, and you look like the kind of guy I want to go with," he said, extending his hand. Dr. Dave Griswell, a Vietnam-era Army veteran and emergency room doctor in DC, became our seventh team member. Finally, in a cramped, sparsely furnished apartment in a nondescript building in Santo Domingo, we met number eight: Jim Boynton, a Catholic Jesuit brother, who had driven across the border from Haiti to pick us up and serve as our guide. Brother Jim, as he was affectionately called, had only been in Haiti for three months on a Jesuit rotation to teach, and now found himself the fixer for a ragtag group of military veterans and medical professionals—half of whom had only been acquainted for the better part of an afternoon.

Now eight members strong, our team had doubled in size—still small, but our rapid growth had reaffirmed our belief that we could have an impact far and above our meager size and resources. The very next day, just four days after the earthquake had killed over one hundred thousand people, we loaded into the backs of trucks and crossed into one of the most dangerous disaster zones of the twenty-first century. Team Rubicon, such as it was, had launched its first mission.

The team that crossed the border into Haiti that day—not to mention the way in which it had been assembled—was unique. Most of its members were not deliberately selected, had no prior experience working together, and had yet to clearly define their roles and responsibilities. Still, that team had a high impact under the most extreme of circumstances, saving dozens of lives and treating countless injuries. Why? Because we had an aligned passion, were willing to sacrifice enormously for a common goal, and faced circumstances that demanded we do exactly that.

In a world where the future of most industries is uncertain, and advances in technology are changing everything in the blink of an eye, teams like these are critical to business success. After all, despite the myth of the solitary entrepreneur changing the world from his college dorm room, the lone soldier racing into the line of fire and singlehandedly taking down enemy forces, or the star player saving the game at the clutch moment, in reality, it is the rare individual who can tackle mighty things all by him- or herself. Bill Gates had Paul Allen. Mark Zuckerberg had a house full of coders. Tom Brady has a world-class offensive line and great wide receivers. The man that killed bin Laden was inserted by helicopter pilots and had his back covered by other Navy SEALs. Selecting and cultivating great teams rarely happens through chance, as it did in the above story; instead, it happens through careful thought and deliberate action. Whatever professional goal you aspire to, if you are going to put it all on the line—whether by starting a new business or trying to succeed within a struggling one—you'll be well served by surrounding yourself with value-added individuals and uniting them into a high-impact team.

So, now that you've learned how to prepare yourself—your mind, your body, and your spirit—for high-impact leadership, we're going to look at how to create the kinds of teams that have the most impact when the stakes are highest. Because whatever type of organization you work for, and whatever position you hold, you can't Take Command without the right people alongside you.

HIGH-IMPACT TEAMS

Before we can talk about building high-impact teams, we first need to understand what exactly a team is. Even if it seems obvious, bear with me for a minute while we establish a working definition: *A team is a group of individual egos, united in pursuit of a common mission or goal, often forgoing personal advancement and comfort for the sake of the whole.* Assuming we agree with this definition, teams require three things: individuals, a common goal, and a willingness of the individuals to sacrifice for that goal. Teams can be as large as a three-hundred-person sales force, or as small as the original Team Rubicon. Beyond the business sphere, a nation is a team; it is a group of individual citizens, subjugating certain individual rights and liberties (like the freedom to yell "fire" in a crowded theater, or to steal from one's neighbors) to a common goal (civil order). On the other end of the spectrum, a marriage is also a team; it is two individuals sacrificing individual freedoms (in my case, watching football twenty hours per week during NFL season) for a common goal or good (love and happiness).

What is a high-impact team (HIT)? A true HIT is defined by some special internal characteristics along with some environmental ones. First, a HIT must be faced with a daunting task or opportunity with high stakes—the chance to turn around a failing inner-city school, or make a new scientific breakthrough, or commercialize a radical new technology—in other words, a mission for which there is a high cost of failure, but also the potential for huge reward. That is the environmental factor. Next come the unique internal characteristics. To have the potential to achieve the highest possible impact, the team must be foolish enough to think it can make a change, daring enough to try, and persistent enough to have a chance.

Foolishness, daring, and persistence—these are the ingredients of a high-impact team. Many leaders will cringe and say, "I don't want any fools on my team." Given the right context, I'd agree. However, when I use the term "foolish," I use it to refer to the dreamers—to those who look at problems and conjure only solutions, who look at obstacles and see only opportunity, who don't ask why, but rather why not. Furthermore, high-impact teams require daring. Dreaming the solution or seeing the opportunity is only worth a shit if you dare to push the boat off the shore and sail toward it. Too often, incredible ideas and innovations go unmaterialized because teams lack daring. Finally, we require persistence. Calvin Coolidge said it best when he stated:

> Nothing in the world can take the place of Persistence. Talent will not; nothing is more common than unsuccessful men with talent. Genius will not; unrewarded genius is almost a proverb. Education will not; the world is full of educated derelicts. Persistence and determination alone are omnipotent. The slogan "Press On" has solved and always will solve the problems of the human race.

Persistence has the potential to pull teams through friction and past obstacles, beyond failure and toward success.

Show me a team that has succeeded despite odds stacked against them, and I will show you a group that doesn't know the definition of *quit*.

All right, so that's what high-impact teams are and consist of, but how do you build them? Well, over the last decade I've joined, led, or built a number of high-impact teams, and along the way I've learned five incredible lessons. Some I learned while following, others while leading; some while succeeding, others while failing. I've followed on teams running missions deep in Taliban-controlled territory; observed team captains lead teams into college football's most hostile stadiums; built and led teams of volunteers into some of the century's worst catastrophes; and been a part of teams building and bringing new technologies to market. Given that range, I'm convinced that these five principles for building high-impact teams transcend industry, rank, and function.

Know Your Role in the Field

Barry Alvarez, former head coach of the Wisconsin Badgers football team, had this as a mantra. "Know your role," he would tell the players and staff repeatedly throughout the season. "Know where you fit in, know how your contribution adds to the greater whole. More important, know and appreciate the roles of those around you." For Coach Alvarez, this principle had two components, which can be summed up in two questions: (1) What is my role, and how does that role fit in and contribute to the success of the team? (2) What is the role of everyone else involved in this organization, from the starters to the equipment managers, and how does their role contribute to the success of the team?

As individuals, it is critical that we know the difference between the role we *want* and the role we *have*. At Wisconsin I wanted my role to be that of an offensive starter, but the role I had was a backup. So while it was critical that I maintained the initiative, work ethic, and attitude of a starter in my pursuit of earning that starting spot, it could never come at the expense of playing my supporting role. I remember that as a backup I once had to swallow my pride and tutor a younger, albeit more talented, player named Joe Thomas. Even though Joe was competing for the same job I wanted, since I had been on the team longer my coach asked me to mentor him on the playbook—which I did, because it was my role.

In business, no matter how high we rise in a company or organization, we're going to be asked to play numerous roles, and we may not like them all. Some we might think are beneath us; others may simply distract us from pursuing the roles we want. Is your company doing some restructuring that requires you to cede leadership responsibilities to someone else and take over some administrative functions? Have you been asked to participate in a multifunctional team that requires you to support rather than direct? Having the humility to accept and excel in these situations will not only benefit the team; ultimately these sacrifices will get noticed and lead you to greater opportunities down the line.

The second component of Coach Alvarez's wisdom is

just as important in business. In order for teams to function effectively, each member must understand and appreciate the functions of other members—and how it affects them. This can be done through active communication, but it's not enough to simply explain what each team member does, and why it is important; more often, getting a true understanding of others' roles requires deliberately exposing ourselves to each other's daily work situation.

I recently spoke to all the administrators in the Milwaukee Public Schools system at the yearly kickoff meeting. They had brought me in to discuss this very topic—building high-impact teams. While discussing this portion of team building—knowing roles—I asked the audience, most of them school principals, who among them had ridden the school bus to work within the last year. Not a single person raised his or her hand. I then asked them if they felt that bullying and violence on the bus ride to and from school contributed to a child's inability to concentrate in the classroom. A series of nodding heads confirmed my assumption. I then told them two things: One, if you have not communicated to your bus drivers the critical role they play in a child's ability to have a peaceful learning environment, how would they know? And two, if you have not ridden the bus within the last year, how can you take informed steps to solve the issue?

By not effectively communicating to the bus drivers their critical role in a child's education, the administrators were missing out on a tremendous opportunity to empower those teammates to be a part of the solution. And by not putting themselves forward and exposing themselves to the point of friction, the administrators were oblivious to the day-to-day challenges those drivers faced in preventing bullying and violence—and how to overcome them.

The act of defining and informing can be particularly challenging at Team Rubicon, where we deploy mostly volunteers. Since, unlike typical employees, these first responders are donating their time and effort without expectation of monetary reward, they often come with a preconceived idea of what role they would like to play in the response. Their thought process is, "I'm willing to give of my time, so I should be able to choose what role I fill on this team. If not, then I won't go." To combat this occasional mentality, our leaders must be supremely effective and empathetic communicators. They must pull aside the volunteer who has been selected to help with administrative duties at the operations base—instead of being assigned the preferred role of helping out with search-and-rescue or home demolition—and convince that person that the role they'll play in admin is far more impactful. Typically the sell isn't what the volunteer will get out of it personally, but rather what the larger team will reap as a result. You'll likely hear our leaders say, "The team really needs you to play this role even if it's not quite as fulfilling, and if you'll do it, we'll be able to get those fifty volunteers standing over there out to the field faster and more effectively," before you'll hear, "You're going to love it!" But because our members are so committed to sacrificing their own individual needs for the good of the collective mission, this generally does the trick.

Of course, we also have great regional managers so dedicated to the mission that they volunteer to come to Los

Angeles instead of the disaster zone, specifically so they can provide support in that administrative role. These volunteers truly understand what roles need to be played to achieve mission success, and they're incredible. The added bonus is that these volunteers gain a unique perspective and are able to see all of the amazing work that goes on behind the scenes to make these operations happen. They are then able to go and educate other volunteers; this communication has proven critical to breaking down perceived headquarters and regional barriers.

In many ways, this is similar to how some companies rotate managers across departments and locations. Certainly there's an element of cross-training involved, but it's as much an effort to cross-pollinate cultures and build trust. So be sure to think about ways that you can expose various members of your team to different components of what your team or organization does. While it may meet resistance at first, it will undoubtedly pay dividends in what you can collectively accomplish.

Build a Level of Trust You'd Go to Battle With

When I was on tour in Afghanistan, it was not uncommon for my sniper team to encounter the following scenario. Our six-man unit would be tasked with running a mission into insurgent-controlled territory, far beyond the immediate reach of traditional ground troops. We would be asked to spend a few days observing enemy activity or movements, and if necessary, compromise our position by taking some precision shots. If compromised, we would have to rely on our supporting units to roll out into a firefight to retrieve us, and possibly even call in air support from foreign NATO pilots who barely spoke English.

What was it that enabled six men, lightly armed, to accept such a high-risk proposition? What enabled us to believe that our counterparts, located miles away, would be willing to jump into the line of fire and risk their lives in our order to save ours? What could possibly make us comfortable with calling in an air strike that would have one-thousand-pound bombs dropped within a hundred yards of our position, by a pilot we'd never met and who didn't even speak our language? The answer is *trust*. The military, in all its manifestations, is a culture built upon unwavering trust. This trust is inculcated in the Marine Corps from the moment a recruit steps on the yellow footprints at boot camp, and stays with you until you take off the uniform for the final time, whether that's four or twenty-four years later.

Many leaders and organizations give lip service to the notion of trust. But trust isn't something that can be instilled through a one-time company retreat or team-building event, or written into a corporate mission statement. Instead, trust must be *actively* built across three areas, by ensuring that (1) all individuals have prepared themselves fully for the task at hand; (2) all individuals have the same, aligned goals; and (3) that each member is willing to sacrifice some part of him- or herself (in the military this is that person's life; in business it might be that person's holiday plans or bonus check) for the good of the team. Trust, in other words, is built across the four "TRs":

Trust = Training + Transparency + Trial & Tribulation

The first, training, is the bedrock of trust. But it's not enough for your team members to simply receive some training; on high-impact teams, each member not only receives training, they all receive *a common training*. In the Marine Corps, as with every developed military force in the world, every member, whether a cadet or a general, goes through nearly the exact same basic training. This consistency assures each member that every other person they encounter has at least some basic level of skill, determination, and culture. Uniform training indoctrinates team values, serves as a filter for those unable to meet basic requirements, and creates a shared common ground. It creates standards and ensures they're met across diverse and far-flung units within organizations such as NATO—so our sniper team on the ground knows that a Danish pilot will follow the same close air-support protocol that a US pilot would, and is able to trust that they will be competent in their execution and courageous in their willingness to expose themselves to danger on our behalf.

Common training is also the cornerstone of many of the most successful and resilient companies. Ask associates at ten different McKinsey offices how to approach a client's problem, and those associates will cite precisely the same methodology. Join the team at Zappos and you'll soon learn that every single employee, regardless of their role, goes through the same basic training.

Transparency, which will be discussed in more detail in a later chapter, is equally critical to building trust. This means being open and honest with your team about the risks they face, so they can trust that when the time comes to jump into the line of fire, they aren't caught off guard. Prior to crossing the border into Haiti, for example, I pulled the original eight members of Team Rubicon together and laid the situation bare: We were going into an unstable country with limited resources and virtually no support. I reiterated one last time that I could not guarantee their safety, only that I would place it above my own.

It is important to note that leaders cannot cultivate transparency unless they push themselves out among the troops to converse with them openly. Whether an Army captain dropping into foxholes on the front lines, or the Milwaukee Public Schools official riding the school bus, or a manager doing a couple of shifts in the call center or on the factory floor, leaders must lead from the front. At Team Rubicon this has actually been made mandatory: No team leader goes out on a mission without spending time "in the trenches." That means that when William and I go out to places like Moore, Oklahoma, after the devastating tornadoes there, we are swinging axes and shovels with our volunteers and sweating alongside them. It's only then that the troops trust that you understand their situation and challenges, and have their interests at heart.

Finally, trust generally requires trial and tribulation. What does this mean? You'll often hear a football coach, after winning the first eight games of the season only to lose number nine, state that the loss will ultimately make his team better. While no fan likes to hear this, there's an element of truth to it. Disappointments like these force individuals to band together and form stronger bonds; in fact, they are necessary. We see this in all elements of society: fraternity and sorority hazing; crucibles at the end of military basic training; grueling twice-a-day practices in athletics; painful internships at banks or consultancies during business school; and so on.

Team Rubicon was forged in a pretty fierce fire. Our initial mission to Haiti thrust us into a situation that immediately required trust; even among individuals who had only known each other for twenty-four hours. Luckily, among the medics and military veterans—no strangers to trial and tribulation—there was an inherent trust born of common training and prior experience under fire; we further cultivated that trust through transparent leadership; and finally, the shared trials of our situation cemented it.

But assuming your line of work doesn't take you to Third World countries immediately after epic disasters, how do you leverage trial and tribulation in your own line of work to build trust? Believe it or not, creating, or magnifying, trials and threats is an age-old trick that's been used by leaders since the beginning of time. Anyone who has had to rally a group knows that nothing sets a team on fire like "us versus them." It is the classic underdog theory that has won wars, turned around teams, transformed flailing companies into forces to be reckoned with, and catapulted struggling professionals to the tops of their fields. David versus Goliath. Barbarians at the gate. There is nothing like the threat of a bigger and badder competitor to motivate teams and individuals to harness their fullest potential. For the startup entrepreneur, that threat might be skeptical investors, or a new market entrant; for the product division leader at a consumer goods company it might be internal competition; for the district attorney it might be the lawyer from the white-shoe law firm, etc.

When tapping into this wellspring of drive and motivation, be careful not to overplay the threats you face, but do make sure that everyone on your team knows that threats to their existence (in a professional sense) are everywhere. If you're Apple (or a fledging start-up with dreams of becoming the next Apple), there's nothing wrong with putting the Microsoft logo on a bull's-eye in the break room.

Passion Trumps Talent, but Culture Is King

If you are in the fortunate situation of being able to choose your team, you're in luck. Jim Collins, the esteemed business author, devotes a large portion of his books to building strong teams—or, as he puts it, getting the right people on the bus, the wrong people off, and ultimately people in the right seats. As Team Rubicon has grown, we've had to carefully select whom to bring onto the core team. In the early stages, this meant a few critical leaders in a small circle at the top, but we've increasingly expanded to more than twenty full-time employees, sixty regional managers, and more than one hundred state coordinators. As we've grown, we've made many mistakes and learned a few lessons, but one rule has always been maintained: Passion trumps talent, but culture is king.

Recall the Calvin Coolidge quote at the beginning of this chapter: *Nothing in the world can take the place of Persistence. Talent will not; nothing is more common than unsuccessful men with talent.* Don't get me wrong, passion and talent are not mutually exclusive. In fact, there's nothing better than a talented person with incredible passion—these are the people that change the world. But faced with a choice, we would take passion over talent any day. Why? Because passion equals persistence, and persistence will overcome anything.

But while passion might be enough to achieve high impact for individuals, if a high-impact *team* is what you're after, then culture is king. Simply put, your culture is your organization's lifeblood. It is what drives decisions in the absence of orders; it is what maintains direction when leaders inevitably move on; it is what makes people excited when their alarm clock goes off on Monday morning. If my experience working on teams as unusual as the Wisconsin Badgers, the Sniper Platoon, and Team Rubicon has taught me anything, it's that if your goal is to recruit the most passionate *and* talented people, your culture needs to be unique.

Still, simply building a unique culture isn't enough if everyone on your team doesn't embrace it fully. In other words, you can find the most talented and passionate person in the world, but if they don't fit your culture, you simply cannot bring them on board. You can't ever compromise on culture. Period.

I'll be the first to admit that hiring in this way is not always easy. At Team Rubicon we were recently searching for a candidate for a new position, a digital engagement associate. This person was going to be responsible for creating all the content across all our digital platforms, and engaging our community of supporters in online conversations. Basically, this person was going to become the voice of Team Rubicon. We interviewed dozens of candidates who had exceptional résumés and demonstrated outstanding passion for veterans' causes, but after three months and countless "final" rounds of interviews, we still found ourselves without the right one. Finally, after another "final-*final*" round of interviews, I stated in exasperation, "That's it, we're going to select one of these three. They're all qualified, they're all likeable, they're all adequate."

William and Mike Lee, our communications coordinator, looked at me in disgust. "How can you say that, Jake? You're going to compromise on a position that is going to have to convey our message to the world? No. We're scrapping them all and starting over tomorrow. We are going to search until we find someone that inspires us." Slightly ashamed, I grudgingly agreed. Forty-eight hours later we received a cover letter (from a Wisconsin Badger, no less) that conveyed the passion, talent, and culture we were looking for. We got her on the phone that day and, five minutes into the interview, William scribbled on a piece of paper, "I want her on the team," stood up, and walked out of the room.

That's how you build a high-impact team!

As important as adding members to the team is, removing members can be just as critical. We're all human, and we're all bound to make mistakes—this is particularly true in hiring. The moment you discover that you've made a mistake—that a person you thought was going to be a key fit turns out to be a cultural cancer—you have to cut that person out. This can often be hard to do; after all, if you're like most leaders you will probably have forged some connection with that person and feel a profound sense of responsibility for that person and his or her family. However, you have to look at it in the larger context. It's entirely too easy for a single person to destroy the workplace atmosphere, and the higher the stakes, the more damage one bad apple can wreak, especially on a close-knit team. We've made mistakes like this at Team Rubicon, and as hard as the decision is to eliminate someone, the rest of the office feels immediately that a weight has been lifted.

Embrace Innovation and Change

In today's fast-paced, high-stakes business environment, good teams know how to adapt. But high-impact teams do more than simply adapt to the winds of change in their company or industry; they iterate, innovate, and evolve constantly. I'll make a quick distinction between adaptation and innovation: Adaptation is reactive; it means responding to changing tides defensively, often when it's too late. Innovation, on the other hand, is proactive; it means anticipating which way the tide will turn and preparing to respond quickly. But just as adaptation does not equal innovation, nor are innovation and change the same thing. Innovation is the spark, and change is the flame. Innovation is an idea, one that is most often discovered nearest the source of a problem. Innovation happens on the front lines of business and is bottom-up. Change takes that innovation and adopts it organization-wide. It requires top-down endorsement and effort.

For organizations and teams to be effective when the stakes are highest, they must do both well. How?

First, in order for innovation to become a part of the culture, leaders must communicate to team members that it is not only okay, but that it is expected. Employees and team members are often fearful of innovating or, worse, reluctant to communicate a new idea for fear that they'll be "rocking the boat." Only if innovation has been indoctrinated in the culture can it take hold. For instance, everyone has heard of Google's famed "20 percent time": their engineers are allowed, and expected, to work on non-assigned projects during 20 percent of their workweek. Examples of this type of innovative atmosphere abound. Take, for instance, Atlassian, another software company, which encourages engineers and coders to take what they call "FedEx Days," or twenty-four-hour periods to work on pet projects. The catch, however, is that just like FedEx, they have to deliver something within twenty-four hours. No pressure!

Innovation and change can only go so far, however, until they are adopted and implemented on the widest scale. In order for this to happen, leaders must identify innovations within their organization and then convince the organization as a whole to buy into them. Luckily, if you've filled your organization and your teams with the kinds of people described above, this won't be as difficult as it sounds.

Once those key innovations have been identified, the first critical step is to actively build coalitions that will support the change. These coalitions must contain a cross-section of the organization, and have individuals from all its various arms, departments, and respective leadership tiers represented. Leaders should also focus on bringing in unlikely supporters—perhaps the person who was most staunchly opposed to the previous initiative, or the person who has the most to lose from making the change. It's important that these not simply be flag-waving, rah-rah coalitions, but people who will actually lead the change through action.

Second, the leader has to craft the argument for change. This argument has a few required components:

1. What makes this change necessary? What is the pain?
2. How will this change alleviate that pain?
3. How will this change impact each individual, each team, and the organization as a unit?
4. What does the organization look like in [insert timeline] if it refuses to adopt this change? What does it stand to lose by not taking action?

The most critical components of this argument are points 3 and 4. Humans are naturally resistant to change (although you should make a person's willingness or ability to change and adapt a conscious decision point in your hiring process), and are also naturally self-preserving—their first reaction is to wonder how a change to the status quo will impact them personally (a true statement, no matter how deliberate you are in cultivating a team culture). As a result, it is imperative that a leader effectively and transparently communicates "what this means for you." Also, keep in mind that arguing what an organization stands to gain through action is far less effective than arguing what an organization, or individual, stands to *lose* through *inaction*.

The third and final step a leader must take to adopt major change is to create an echo chamber that assures that the change, its importance, and its progress are front and center always. The change, if crafted carefully, should become a rallying cry—an organization-wide initiative that everyone can get behind (probably building some trust along the way!).

In early 2013 we made sweeping changes throughout Team Rubicon in this very way. Five months earlier, in the midst of Hurricane Sandy, we discovered that our loose organizational structure, lack of formalized emergency management training, and slack policies were exposing our organization to too much risk. We knew what changes we had to make, but also knew that those changes would meet resistance among some "old guard" Team Rubicon leaders who had been around since the beginning.

So we followed the formula above. Prior to holding a major leadership summit, I spent time building a coalition of influencers with representatives from all the field offices in all the different regions, cuing them into the changes that were coming, and securing their buy-ins. Next, we carefully crafted the argument for why these drastic changes were necessary—focusing on the impact the changes were going to have on the team as well as on each individual (mandates for minimum training, increased roles and responsibilities, tighter policies), and on the hazards the organization would face if the changes weren't enacted (greater liability, failure to reach its full potential). Finally, at the leadership summit, we crafted our echo chamber by launching the program with a call to action to "burn the boat." *Burning the boat* refers to the general who, upon leading his army across the treacherous seas and landing on the enemy's shore, orders his men to burn their boats so they are left with no option but to move forward and succeed. At Team Rubicon, we knew that the changes we wanted to implement were necessary for the organization to achieve its highest impact. So upon explaining the current situation, the new changes that were coming, how they affected each individual and the success of the company, we called upon our leaders to burn the boat. Any leader who wanted to move forward with us could, and was expected to do so with unrelenting enthusiasm. Others who were less convinced were asked to stay on shore.

Build a Brand That Inspires

This chapter started by defining a team as a group of individual egos, sacrificing for a common mission or goal, often forgoing personal advancement and comfort for the sake of the whole. Thus far we have focused on how to find, recruit, and motivate these individuals—how to communicate to them their roles and importance, how to build trust among them, how to encourage them to innovate and change. We come now to the last point, which is about another component of high-impact teams: being united in the mission and the indistinguishable "whole." If you build a brand that truly inspires, this will foster the highest level of loyalty and commitment to your organization and its shared goals.

These days, the word "brand" gets misused a lot. You may not even think your company or team has a brand—or even needs one. But in truth, a brand is simply whatever it is your company stands for, and *every* company or organization stands for something, whether you know it or not.

But a brand is more than a corporate identity—more than a logo or font or slogan. A brand is more than a product. A brand is a mission, an ethos, and a culture. Brands are not developed on paper and there is no surefire formula to get them right. Brands are not one-size-fits-all, and when attempts are made to copy others', they tend to fail. Nor can a brand be an afterthought. From the very inception of an organization, brand building must be baked into every single decision.

I would argue—although I'm biased—that the Marine Corps has one of the best brands in the entire world. The Marine Corps has developed an identity, a culture—and a sense of pride in that culture—that is unparalleled, even among its sister services. It is not uncommon for Marines to express loyalty to their Corps before their country.

Motorists driving down the highways of America might assume that the Marine Corps is the largest of all the service branches, if judging by the volume of bumper stickers. They'd probably be shocked to find out it is by far the smallest.

It's no coincidence that the strength of the Marine Corps brand is directly correlated to its lifespan. I recently met with a group of Army colonels assigned to a new Army initiative called Soldier for Life, essentially a rebranding effort the Army is conducting internally to try to elicit greater feelings of pride, ownership, and lifetime association from soldiers during and after their service. Ten minutes into the meeting I blurted out, "You guys are trying to do in twelve or twenty-four months what the Marine Corps has done for two hundred and thirty years!" They sheepishly admitted that I was right.

How did the Marine Corps achieve its legendary brand? It certainly didn't do it with marketing dollars. It did it with consistent messaging that articulated its core values, actions that backed up its words, and the careful cultivation of loyalty. The result is a brand that inspires young men and women to do incredible things, not the least of which is to sign up for combat jobs during a decade-long war.

At Team Rubicon we have taken many cues from the Marine Corps in building our brand. We use consistent language to describe our values and mission—and then back that up with action. We shy away from individualism (recall the Army's "Army of One" campaign?) and focus on the team. We pride ourselves on going where others don't dare go, and doing jobs that others won't do. We brag that we can do more with less. On missions, we make sure that team members know they are judged by how dirty they are at the end of a long day. We value integrity, honor, and respect, but don't pretend to be perfect.

I believe one of the reasons our men and women actively volunteer to follow us into some of the most ravaged and dangerous disaster zones the world has ever seen is because we've done all of the above, and communicated it effectively, both externally and internally. We have created a literal army of brand ambassadors, and as a result our brand no longer lives at our headquarters in Los Angeles; it lives on the chests of tens of thousands of members across the country who have been inspired to lead and serve in their communities and make sacrifices for the sake of others. At one point we thought we'd measure the power of our brand by the number of fans we had on Facebook, until we realized that we could measure by the number of people who were actually tattooing our logo onto their bodies. It was at that point, after seeing dozens of volunteers express their loyalty through permanent body ink, that we knew we were building a brand with staying power—literally. That's the difference between a team that will follow you into the line of fire and one that will crumble under pressure when the stakes are highest.

I stated at the beginning of this section that there's no formula for building a brand, and that is largely true. But there are a few things you should always be asking yourself as you build and develop the culture and brand of your team. What is my mission? What is my vision? What do we stand for? What change would we sacrifice everything for in order to make it happen? If you can answer and communicate that last one, and you have people on board who are foolish enough to think they can do it, daring enough to try, and persistent enough to have a chance, that's when you know you've built a brand—and, indeed, a team—that can achieve the highest level of impact.

Whether your team has two people or two hundred, whether they're volunteers or employees, and whether they work in finance or retail or anything in between, if you can unite them in a shared mission and convince them that they are capable of great things, that is when you know you are well on your way to building a high-impact team.

MISSION BRIEF

- A high-impact team is one that is faced with a high-stakes mission; in other words, an opportunity for which there is a high cost of failure, but also the potential for huge reward.
- Foolishness, daring, and persistence are the unique and necessary characteristics of a high-impact team.
- As the leader of a high-impact team, you must know not only your role but the roles of those around you.
- Trust is built through training, transparency, and trial and tribulation.
- Culture is king—no amount of passion or talent can make up for a poor cultural fit.

- As the leader of an HIT, it is your job to embrace innovation and make sure that a culture of change is widely adopted throughout all levels. This requires building coalitions and crafting convincing arguments that make the case for change compelling.
- If you build a brand that inspires, it will unite your team in their commitment and loyalty to your organization's mission and goals, building bonds that endure when the pressure is mounting and a lot is on the line.

LESSON 3

Establish Transparency; Demand Accountability

Diligently I lifted the little boy's leg as Mark Hayward continued to slice away gangrenous tissue that was threatening the child's life. Pausing for a moment, I adjusted my gloved hands in order to put less pressure on the exposed tibia protruding from where the brave boy's ankle was supposed to be. "What do you say, Mark? Is he going to keep the rest of his leg?"

"Hard to say," Mark said matter-of-factly, as was his style. Mark had been an Army Special Forces medic in a prior life. "The condition of this tissue concerns me; it's obvious it hasn't been tended to since the quake. If his blood is septic, he'll need to worry about more than his leg."

It was January 19, seven days after the massive Haiti earthquake, and we were helping to run the only operating hospital in Port-au-Prince. On the table in front of me lay a young boy, likely only nine years old, bravely whimpering while Mark cut hunks of infected flesh off of his crushed limb. The emergency room was overcrowded and clambering with commotion—doctors running in and out, patients wailing and begging to be seen, and Team Rubicon volunteers deliberately moving from table to table triaging patients and providing any possible treatment. Amid all the chaos, I looked back down at the little boy, gently patted the sweat off of his brow, and smiled in an attempt to comfort him.

Suddenly my partner, William McNulty, appeared at my side, grabbing me on the shoulder. "What's up, man?" I asked, glancing upward.

"A few things. The team of doctors I arranged out of Chicago is en route and will arrive in two waves; the first ones will be here in less than three hours. They have two tons of medical supplies with them, so I'm working with François, our interpreter, on getting some more tap-tap trucks to help transport everything. Second, the guy in charge over across the courtyard is saying the hospital is running out of water—"

"Don't they know there's enough water at the airport for an army?" I interrupted with frustration.

"Yeah, they're concerned about the security of getting from there to here," William responded.

I shook my head in frustration. The situation on the ground in Port-au-Prince was grim—hundreds of thousands were feared dead, an equal number were seriously wounded, and bodies were still buried in rubble. To make matters worse, Haiti was one of the poorest, most corrupt nations on earth, and emergency services and infrastructure were nearly nonexistent. With limited food and water, there was a real risk that the surviving populace would move from unstable to violent. Despite a massive world-wide relief effort that was dumping hundreds of tons of supplies into the Port-au-Prince airport, bureaucracy was preventing those supplies from getting where they needed to go—like our hospital.

William shrugged his shoulders. "Tell me about this little guy," he asked, changing subjects and smiling at the young boy. "What's his status?"

"Good chance he is going to lose his leg," I responded, "but he's a brave little dude. Hasn't shed a single tear the whole time Mark's been hacking away at that gangrene. Mark, can you ask him what his name and age are?" Mark, through his limited French and Creole, managed to get the child's name and age.

"Pierre, age ten . . ." William's voice trailed off as he typed hurriedly on his BlackBerry's keyboard. Then, looking up, he stepped back and raised the phone in front of his eyes to snap a picture of the chaos around us. "There, I'll put that up on the blog and social media. We'll let everyone know that not only are people dying from their wounds, but soon they'll be at risk of dying from dehydration because nobody is taking action. We'll shed light on this shit-show."

SHEDDING LIGHT

Shed light. What William meant was that we needed to create transparency—to hold those active in the response, including ourselves, accountable for each and every decision and action. It wasn't about laying blame or creating a witch hunt, only about ensuring that results were being achieved. William and I felt a particularly strong need to demonstrate real results on our first mission in Haiti. Remember, Team Rubicon didn't exist the week prior to that moment in Port-au-Prince. Just days before, when we'd decided to organize a team of military veterans and doctors to respond to the earthquake, we had to rely on the goodwill of friends and family to support the effort—we had no funds raised, no government backing, no corporate donors, not even a charitable, tax-exempt status. As money began coming in to my personal PayPal account, we pledged to each of those donors that we would (1) do more with less, forgoing any luxury or convenience for the sake of the mission; (2) document, to every extent possible, all our actions taken on the ground in real time through a blog and social media; and (3) account for every dollar in a thorough after-action review. At that point we had no idea if our mission would succeed or fail. After all, what we were doing—dropping a bunch of vets and medics into a disaster zone with virtually no supplies, no real knowledge of the region, and no formal disaster relief experience—was pretty unprecedented, and results were uncertain at best. But what we *could* promise our donors in return for their support and faith in us, at the very least, was that we'd provide transparency in our actions.

From the moment we landed in the Dominican Republic, to the time we rolled into Port-au-Prince a few hours later, all the way through the final day in Haiti, we provided our donors—and anyone else who wanted to look—a clear window through which they could observe every aspect of our operations—including how we spent each and every charitable dollar. It was, we dare claim, a pioneering use of new media to "tell a story," and to keep us accountable for our decisions and our actions—and for the decisions and actions of those around us. More important, it forced us to be scrupulously conscious of how we deployed our limited manpower and resources; it kept us honest. This deliberate effort to be transparent in everything we do has played a huge role in our early success—in more ways than one.

The Power of Trust

I believe that transparency is critical on two fronts: externally, to the people you serve, be they charitable donors, corporate clients, or retail customers; and internally, to your team and employees. At TR, we actively use social media to create unparalleled external transparency—to shed light on all our activities and abolish the informational barriers of traditional giving in disaster relief efforts. In your work, external transparency might mean completely leveling with your investors about your company's current financial crunch; or readily admitting that you've just discovered your new product is contaminated, instead of waiting for a news story to break. Whatever it is, you too can use social media to communicate key information about your business to customers and stakeholders.

The other type of transparency, internal, is just as critical to organizations that face extreme and uncertain circumstances. Good leaders in nimble and fast-paced organizations not only clearly communicate the importance of transparency; they strive to demonstrate it throughout all levels of the organization. These leaders don't hide the sometimes brutal realities the team is facing, whether a potentially hostile takeover or a diminishing cash runway. They do this because they know that transparency creates trust, and when a team has trust (as discussed in the previous chapter about building high-impact teams), they will sacrifice individual desires for the sake of the whole without hesitation. No matter what type or size team you lead, if you want to be the kind of leader who inspires others to follow you into the line of fire, it's up to you to create unparalleled internal *and* external transparency using every tool available.

External

Our efforts in Haiti to create absolute transparency between our on-the-ground activities and our donors established two things. One, it served as a system of checks and balances for the way in which we operated—where we went, whom we helped, and how we spent the charitable dollars that were flowing our way. When making important decisions like these, it was not uncommon for William and I to have a brief discussion around the question "How would our donors perceive this decision?"

Two, this transparency created an enormous amount of trust between our team and our supporters—and because of the media we used, that trust quickly went viral. Not only were we totally transparent about how we spent our—that is, our donors'—money, we held ourselves accountable in another way, too, by doing something we had never seen done before: We offered our donors back the portion of their money that we didn't use in Haiti. *What? A nonprofit offering to return a donation?* See, after returning from Haiti, William and I faced a choice. We had raised money well in excess of what we'd spent, and had tens of thousands of dollars left over. However, it didn't feel right to use money given for Haiti to explore this Team Rubicon "experiment" further (remember, we never intended to start an organization—only to help in Haiti). So we sent every single one of our donors an e-mail that outlined how much we raised during the mission and how much we subsequently spent. The e-mail continued to include our vision and plans for the future; how we thought that during our efforts in Haiti we'd discovered something unique—the opportunity to build an organization that could do disaster relief differently, and in a way that engages our returning military veterans. The e-mail ended by stating that we'd happily return the unused, pro rata portion of their donation back to them; but if they elected that we keep it, we'd use it to deploy Team Rubicon the next time there was a disaster.

Our donors were floored. Our e-mail in-box was flooded with gracious notes from supporters stating that so long as we maintained that level of transparency, they would remain long-term supporters of our efforts—and they have. Imagine if other organizations, so often criticized for raising massive amounts of donations only to have little to show their supporters for it, followed suit? Think about how perceptions of those organizations would change if they were completely transparent and open about where each and every dollar was going and why. I will venture to say that opinions of their brands would improve, and they'd likely raise even more money.

Whether you're running a relief organization, a for-profit business, or anything else, there's no greater evangelist for your product or brand than your customers. And indeed, at Team Rubicon we consider our donors to be our customers; and we consider our response missions our product. Every day we come to work our goal is to improve, market, and sell that product, and a commitment to transparency and accountability is a critical part of that marketing strategy. It is baked into all aspects of our brand—and it should be in yours as well. And by the way, you might be wondering, how many donors asked for a portion of their donation back? Well, after Haiti, out of the roughly 1,600 individual donors, one, yes a grand total of one, asked for her donation back. Building irrefutable trust and transparency with our donor (customer) base cost us about seventeen dollars.

For some companies transparency isn't an option—think publicly traded companies and the requirements they have with financial reporting. For others, transparency is a four-letter word—think Apple and its highly secretive nature surrounding new product development. Certainly, when it comes to your company's product development a little cloud of secrecy is well advised, but there are also examples involving Apple that demonstrate they could use a lesson on transparency. Take for instance the public accusations about their manufacturing and labor practices in China. Apple has largely allowed such accusations to go unaddressed, leading to a very vocal backlash in the media and on the blogosphere, and a huge wave of negative PR. True, Apple is one of the strongest and most profitable brand names in the country, but I'm here to bet they could likely galvanize even greater brand loyalty by addressing these claims with absolute transparency.

Hopefully you will never be in a position where as a leader you'll have to accept blame publicly, outside your company; but if you are, you must not hesitate. Some of the largest gaffes in recent corporate history stem from the public outcry when a leader shirked responsibility for public fiascoes. Remember the BP oil spill? Of course you do. Remember the CEO's public apology and promise to right all the wrongs? Nope, because it didn't happen. Instead the public was given a laundry list of excuses, including an attempt to pass the buck onto a subcontractor managing the Deep Horizon well. The public was then treated to the images of Tony Hayward, the BP CEO, on his yacht off the coast of Britain, attempting to escape the public fallout and pressure from the event. True leaders know, and accept, that bearing the ridicule and pressure of mistakes is their cross to bear. Hayward would have served his employees and shareholders far better had he instead flown to the Gulf Coast and put his face in front of a camera, looked the public in the eye, accepted the blame, and delivered a sincere promise to make it right. Instead, his lack of personal fortitude shattered a reputable brand.

But did British Petroleum get anything right? In fact they did. Shortly after the spill, BP positioned a camera at the breach point, and allowed the footage coming back to stream live to the world. It was literally a 24/7 window that showed any concerned citizen just how bad the fiasco was, and didn't allow BP to hide. That's transparency—although in BP's case it was too little, too late.

What steps can you take to achieve this level of trust and transparency for your business or organization? How can you build and engage a base of loyal customers and turn them into evangelists for your brand? In order to make transparency a part of your company's DNA, you have to start at the top.

Internal

What most leaders don't realize is that it's just as important to be transparent about things like the company finances, potential PR stumbles, major organizational changes on the horizon, and so on, within the organization as outside of it. After all, these are the kinds of issues that ultimately affect employees just as much if not more than external stakeholders. Truly effective leaders commit themselves to both forms of transparency, no matter how dire the circumstances. These leaders acknowledge the situation and don't hide from the brutal reality. They work to help their team understand the challenges ahead, and use them as an opportunity to refocus on what tasks are necessary to overcome them. This is critical, because when the stakes are high, team members want to know what is going on behind the curtain, because they have as much at stake as you do. A few years ago, shortly after making a few hires that required people to relocate across the country, Team Rubicon found itself in a growing financial crunch. Our burn rate—the amount of cash that we were "burning" through each month—was increasing, and at the same time fundraising was slowing down. It was a situation that only our director of finance and I had a real grasp on, because of our job responsibilities, but it was something that had obvious implications for everyone on payroll. Many entrepreneurs have faced a similar circumstance—that seed round or Series A you raised is slowly dwindling, and product monetization hasn't happened yet. It's tempting in this situation to keep the information about financial woes close to the chest; don't tell anyone, you think, and hopefully the situation will improve and nobody will have to suffer undue stress.

As our coffers were running out at Team Rubicon—we only had about three months of cash left—it was creating an enormous amount of strain on me. Like the hypothetical entrepreneur above, I felt like I was doing my team a favor by not letting them know about the situation. But then I realized that by trying to shoulder the burden alone, I was too stressed to manage the team effectively, and other tasks of mine were slipping. Finally, I leveled with everyone and clued them in—times were tough, we needed to pull together, but I was confident we'd be okay. The result? Nobody freaked out; we came together and shouldered the burden as a team. One month later Hurricane Sandy hit, and the impact we demonstrated during that response bought us much-needed visibility and credibility with some major corporate sponsors, which made our financial concerns disappear.

The lesson here isn't that transparency will result in windfall accounts at just the right time, but instead that transparency builds trust and galvanizes teams. Just as the transparency we demonstrated with our external supporters during the Haiti earthquake cemented trust and support, internal transparency can do the same.

Transparency doesn't only relate to Armageddon scenarios. Internal transparency is just as important for the mundane. Why is a certain policy being adopted? How or why was a particular decision made? How will this change in direction impact my working hours?

At Team Rubicon, William and I have implemented a number of policies in an effort to generate transparency and convey our commitment to it. Probably the most important and obvious is our open-door policy. At our headquarters any employee, at any time, can enter my office, close the door, and speak freely—without asking permission, without scheduling a block of time. The topics can be anything, but typically range from questions about decisions that have been made to concerns about cultural shifts within the organization, to ideas for how to improve some process or procedure. These policies all extend virtually as well, which is important given that we have such a geographically diverse leadership team. What this means is that all of our sixty nationwide regional managers are able to reach me with any concern or question, day or night, via e-mail or cell phone.

In addition, I've made my work calendar available to anyone that wants to see it. If someone in the organization wants to see what meetings I'm taking, or know why I'm out of the office for a four-hour block on a particular day, they're free to check it out. I want them to know that I have nothing to hide, and that if I'm out for a martini lunch they're invited! This sends an incredibly powerful message that secrets aren't tolerated; that everyone in the company, regardless of their pay grade, deserves to know what is happening at the top.

I also established a sacred block of time every day at 6:30 p.m., Monday through Friday, appropriately called Office Hours (I don't know how I know about office hours; I never visited anyone's office while in college). During Office Hours anyone can access my calendar and schedule time to come talk about anything on their mind—even if it's just to vent. There are only two rules:

1. The problem should always be solved at the lowest point possible in the chain of command. If someone's direct supervisor can handle the problem, he or she should. However, the moment it is obvious that something can't be solved at a lower level and warrants my attention, anyone can raise it to me via phone or e-mail without gaining permission from a superior (more on this policy later).

2. I only accept criticism that is offered along with possible solutions. If someone has not bothered to brainstorm an alternative, then that person is simply being lazy; and in a rapidly growing orga-

nization like ours, where everything is on the line,
laziness can't be tolerated.

Because William and I want to be sure that everyone
feels comfortable raising concerns, we've also adopted a
method for collecting anonymous comments. Every single
e-mail that is sent out to our internal leadership list includes
a link at the bottom soliciting anonymous comments—it's
a catchall that guarantees issues are raised, even if the person raising them is concerned about how it will reflect upon
them. Within a few weeks of adopting the policy, William
and I were made aware, through a series of independent
comments, that one of our leaders was causing a cultural
rift that was threatening to spill over into more widespread
damage. While we'd sensed elements of the concerns, having a method that enabled people to feel comfortable shar-
ing information allowed us to see the entire picture clearly
and take action.

William and I recently brought on board a new chief
operations officer named Ken, an incredible leader who is
extraordinarily committed to transparency. Ken adopted a
new task tracker within our operations team and immediately had it displayed on a television screen that hangs
high on the wall in our bull pen. Now, at all times, everyone in the office can see the tasks each person is working
on, when it should be completed, and, consequently, when
deadlines are not met. I loved the idea, so I asked Ken to
take it further, and now that task tracker is accessible online by any one of our regional managers. We don't want
any secrets at headquarters!

THE EYE OF GOD—
DEMAND ACCOUNTABILITY

So you've established transparency; now what? Now you have to demand accountability. If you don't, all your transparency will have done is highlight problems and demonstrate your unwillingness to address them. If you find yourself a part of or leading a team in an organization that has a lot on the line, it's even more critical that everyone know that accountability is expected—no matter the circumstance. If people see a lack of accountability on the little things—things as innocuous as being late for a meeting, or forgetting to send something to a client, or even forgetting to restock the printer paper—they'll fear that there'll be no accountability when all the chips are on the table.

Just as transparency starts with leadership, so does accountability. A leader must create a culture of accountability by readily admitting failure and assuming the mantle of blame, again both internally and externally. Doing so internally reinforces to staff that you are grounded, humble, and self-aware—all critical to establishing a trusting team. Did a member of your team exercise her right to e-mail you with well-communicated criticism and an alternative for improvement? Be progressive enough to accept the criticism, thank the critic (it helps sometimes to do this in front of others, so that they see that the open-door policy works), and take actions to improve. The antithesis of this type of leader—one who constantly passes the buck, looks for others to blame, or worse, can't admit that failure has occurred—breeds contempt and mistrust.

Did a competitor catch you off-guard with the launch of a new competing product? Accept the blame for not providing your team with better situational awareness of the competitive landscape. The mistakes don't necessarily have to be high-stakes ones; assuming blame can be as simple as apologizing for rescheduling a meeting at the last minute, or for a glitch in the company e-mail system that took longer than it should have to resolve. Even if neither monitoring competitive product launches nor fixing computer issues are your job, if you're the leader, they're all your responsibility. Taking responsibility when the stakes are low is one way to ensure that your team will trust you when the stakes are high.

Once you've set the standard for accountability through your own behavior, it's time to use it to cultivate accountability throughout the culture of your organization. How? You hold those around you to the same standard you hold yourself. Just as your team won't ever see you making excuses for failures, nor should you accept excuses from them when they don't meet a goal. The moment you discover people not maintaining personal accountability, take immediate actions to address it.

I had my first painstaking lesson in accountability long before I cofounded Team Rubicon. In fact, I learned my first lesson about accountability nearly a decade prior, when I first set foot onto the University of Wisconsin varsity football practice field, where I was instantly intimidated by the cavernous stadium, enormous seniors, and fire-breathing coaching staff. Even more intimidating, however, was the giant camera referred to as the "Eye of God." The Eye of

God was not in fact a single video camera but multiple cameras that rested on cranes high above the practice field, carefully positioned to capture every single throw, every single catch, every single play, and every single drill. Every. Single. One.

Knowing that every move we made on the practice field was being recorded was intimidating, but certainly, I remember thinking, we can't possibly watch and review every drill? That evening I found out that, yes, we could; and yes, it would be bad. My position coach on the offensive line was a man named Jim Huber; and Coach Huber was legendary for his ability to make a grown man melt in his seat under a withering barrage of criticism. After each practice, as we reviewed that day's video, Coach Huber would dissect every play in excruciating detail for hours on end, sometimes rewinding a single play more than thirty times to review the actions of each of the five linemen.

But while it was horrible and painful and humiliating at the time, the Eye of God held us accountable for every single move we made on the field. With the Eye of God upon us, not a single detail was overlooked. There was no room for error, and even less room for laziness. As a result, the University of Wisconsin has consistently had more offensive linemen drafted into the National Football League than nearly any other school over the last two decades (no, I wasn't one of them!).

Imagine if you had a similar method of accountability in your place of work. I'm not talking about spyware on your computer to keep track of whether people are spending more time on Facebook than on PowerPoint; or a creepy

IT guy reading through everyone's e-mail looking for vacation photos. I'm talking about holding you and everyone who works for you truly accountable for their performance on each and every task.

When I talk about performance, however, I don't just mean at game time. Performance isn't just about whether you met your sales goals or quarterly projections, or get your reports in on time. When I talk about accountability of performance, I'm talking about both method *and* result. Some leaders dismiss methodology when evaluating performance, and that's a dangerous omission. For these people, performance falls into only two categories:

Bad Result	Good Result

This view is incredibly shortsighted. I think of it as akin to assuming that the eighth-grade basketball phenom who dominates every game is invariably headed to the NBA. Think about it. An early bloomer, he's head and shoulders taller than his peers, and easily scores point after point and grabs rebound after rebound. He refuses to practice his technique because, why would he? He's the best player on the court—he gets results. Soon, however, the rest of his peers grow and mature, and because they invested in and honed their skills (their method) early on, they soon catapult past him onto the varsity team, leaving him in their dust.

It's easy for leaders to focus only on results. Results are measurable and quantifiable in ways that methods often are not. And results are certainly important; not achieving them can cost you your job, the confidence of your investors, or that promotion you're aiming for. However, in today's volatile and unpredictable business environment, where you never know where the next competitor will come from or the next disruption will hit, even more important is establishing a proven methodology, so you'll be ready to face any unexpected challenge that might arise. Establishing and holding people accountable for following consistent methodology—known as "technique" on the athletic field; "standard operating procedure" on the battlefield; "incident management" in the disaster zone—is difficult for leaders, particularly in high-stakes industries or businesses. But it can be done.

First, as I learned all too well from Coach Huber, it requires steely discipline and tedious effort (though, luckily, those following the principles of preparation in the first lesson know that discipline is a skill that can be honed!). All too often, leaders in fast-paced businesses—particularly entrepreneurs—view methodology and procedure as bureaucratic. They see them as the antiquated trappings of the industry titans they are actively trying to topple; the enemy of innovation and progress. What they soon realize, however, is that consistent systems and methods liberate organizations and individuals to work more efficiently and independently. If good methods and systems are in place, and people know they are being held accountable for following them, a culture of trust can flourish; managers don't *have* to be constantly looking over everyone's shoulder to ensure that the work is being done. Good methodology drives positive results not just once or twice—not just this week or this month—but nearly every time it is properly employed. Results follow methods. When we look at the relationship between performance and results, we find a matrix like this:

METHODOLOGY → RESULTS	
Poor → Poor	Poor → Good
Good → Poor	Good → Good

From this matrix we can glean a few important notes. First, it is possible to achieve a good result using poor methodology—just know that it will be inconsistent and short-lived, like the eighth-grade phenom's basketball career. Leaders must never inadvertently confuse a good result with good performance. Perhaps the best example of this was the wildly successful results of the housing securities market leading up to the 2008 crash. Large banks were making money hand-over-fist by creating new collateralized mortgage instruments. At the time nobody was complaining, because the results, it seemed, were making everyone money. A look, however, at the methodology leading to those profits—bundling high-risk home mortgages and underwriting loans to highly unqualified buyers— would have revealed massive flaws. It wasn't long before everyone from the treasury secretary to Joe Homeowner learned that good results driven by bad methodology have a short life.

Alternatively, without accountability, good methodology does not guarantee good results. To look back on a bad result and automatically assume that our methods or assumptions were incorrect is flawed thinking and can result in unnecessary knee-jerk changes that dismantle good systems and cause confusion along the way. It's important to realize that in any high-stakes business situation, even good methodology, impeccably executed, can lead to bad results—that's the nature of risky endeavors. I've seen firsthand how this can play out in the military and in the disaster zone—the perfect attack or response plan, planned with precision, can easily be derailed in the middle of execution by unforeseen aftershocks that crumble infrastructure critical to success. Similarly, the major unforeseen aftershocks that can derail good methodology in high-stakes businesses are numerous: new government regulation; competition from unexpected entrants into the market; a corporate restructuring or takeover; meltdown of financial markets; and many more. Many of us have had the misfortune of having a boss who careens a company's strategy back and forth between two extremes, never sticking with a strategy long enough to truly measure its effects. This type of leader, one who doesn't know his or her own industry well enough to understand that bad results will occasionally happen, can be cancerous for morale.

The point is that developing, testing, refining, and implementing good methodology does not guarantee success, but it guarantees your best *chance* at success. It also inspires confidence within the organization, and confident decision makers can be an organization's ace in the hole when results appear to be taking a bad turn. This is why on the Wisconsin Badgers football team, the Eye of God wasn't just about results—although if you had a bad one, you certainly heard about it—it was about holding us accountable for our method, as well. For example, on any given play, an offensive lineman's assignment is to block a defensive player. Each play used a distinctly different block, and each block had a carefully choreographed footwork technique. On any given play, with any given block, a lineman could win just by using brute strength. But this depended largely on luck; the only way to proactively put yourself in a position for success—though success was never guaranteed—was to use proper technique; and they Eye of God held us all accountable for following that technique. If a block called for an initial six-inch step at a forty-five-degree angle, then an eight-inch step was unacceptable—and the camera would reveal it, regardless of outcome. This rule for measuring good performance must be hard and fast; with no room for leaders to make excuses. As Coach Huber used to eloquently put it, "Excuses are like assholes—everyone has one and they all stink."

The military uses a similar technique to hold people accountable for methodology, called after-action reviews, or AARs, and thorough ones are a hallmark of the military. After any military operation, key leaders will meet to discuss what went right and what went wrong—how were standard operating procedures and tactics applied? Were communication protocols followed? We've adopted the same stringent AAR process at Team Rubicon; and everyone who participates in a mission knows that they'll be subject to a review of their performance on the back end.

The purpose of it is not to diminish morale and point out failures, but rather to identify areas of possible improvement.

We can see incredible examples of resolute focus on accountability in successful businesses all around us. One of the most famous is perhaps Southwest Airlines, which has defied the airline industry's profitability woes year after year. Southwest Airlines was founded on and still operates according to a simple methodology: fly only a single aircraft type to reduce pilot and maintenance costs; service small hubs with short routes; don't assign seats; and have the shortest gate turnaround times in the industry. When Bill Franklin, Southwest's former VP of ground operations, dictated that turnaround times would be ten minutes—at a time when most airlines took nearly an hour—it wasn't just some empty edict; he demanded that this turnaround time be met and that every single employee be held accountable for meeting it. Franklin was reportedly once challenged by a ground crewman who didn't think ten minutes was possible, to which Franklin responded, "If you can't do it I'll fire you and keep firing and firing until I find people who can do it." When deregulation hit, most nationwide carriers were scrambling to cope with the new competitive landscape, shifting methodologies and abandoning time-tested protocols. Southwest, however, stuck to its methodology, determined that results would continue to follow. Follow they did. In 2012, Southwest Airlines achieved its fortieth straight year of profitability, while nearly the entire rest of the airline industry was suffering through bankruptcy.

In today's high-pressure and high-stakes world of business, if we truly value the benefits of unfiltered feedback and transparency, then we as leaders must take deliberate steps to foster an environment that makes it okay for anyone—be they employees, teammates, or customers—to criticize both game-time performance (results) as well as techniques during practice (methods).

The first step is to define both the methods and results desired. Admittedly, this is very difficult for start-ups like Team Rubicon. Start-ups—like any fast-paced businesses—find it hard to define measurable results and set clearly articulated methods, because their terrain is always shifting, and they are always blazing new trails. For example, at Team Rubicon our long-standing goal has been to respond to natural disasters as quickly, efficiently, and safely as possible, while maximizing impact on the ground. But this desired "result" is hard to quantify, especially in places as unpredictable as disaster zones. How fast is quick? How do you measure efficiency—cost per life saved? per mission completed? per volunteer deployed? How do you define "safe"? And so on. However, as you begin to collect more and more data points for your organization, it should become clear what your key performance indicators are.

The challenges of managing all this uncertainty are one of the primary reasons why, as you read earlier, we have taken deliberate steps to establish open-door policies throughout the entire organization, and we've tried to encourage their use as widely as we can. This way, if any one of our 15,000 volunteers spots a method that isn't as safe as it could be, or notices a procedure that isn't delivering efficient results, it's not only that person's right, but their responsibility, to walk up to a team leader or supervisor and hold him or her accountable. It's also why we use online survey tools to solicit anonymous feedback from our key regional leadership—about sixty individuals—on a quarterly basis, giving leaders who might feel uncomfortable speaking up in person the means to be totally transparent about which methods aren't achieving their desired results.

Another excellent way to drive accountability is through competition. Competition, if constructive and friendly rather than cutthroat, naturally breeds accountability because it demands scorekeeping and measurement. At Team Rubicon, we've created competition between our ten geographic regions. Awhile back, we determined that we needed to do a better job of engaging our volunteers and training them between disasters, but we were having a hard time getting the regional managers to emphasize it. So in order to drive accountability, we tied each region's budget to a formula that used engagement and training metrics as inputs, and then produced a regional budget as an output. The formula took into account regional differences like geographic and demographic factors, and normalized them in order to produce a fair competitive landscape. Now we see an increased level of accountability, because the impact is real.

You can implement policies like these too, in your organization. If you have different teams with the same function in your organization—sales teams, implementation teams, etc.—it's a great idea to pit them against one another in a friendly competition; perhaps rewarding the team that signs the most new clients or customers, brings in the highest sales volume, generates the highest conversion rate from their online marketing campaign, comes up with the most viable new product ideas, etc., over a finite period. If there is a tangible reward on the line—paid time off or a bonus—teammates will hold *each other* accountable (after all, no one wants to be the guy who cost his office mate a week's paid vacation) and not think twice that their output is being scrutinized. Consider putting up a leaderboard in the office, so that every day employees are reminded that something is on the line, and see where they fall in the current standings. Provide competition updates at weekly meetings or in companywide e-mails every month. Bottom line? When you talk about accountability, make sure they know you mean it!

THE RIPPLE EFFECT

Finally, once you've infused transparency and accountability throughout the ranks of your team or company, they will continue to ripple outward until they splash up against the people with whom you are ultimately trying to build lasting (and profitable) trust—your customers. When I think of the ultimate example of corporate accountability to customers, I think of the return policy at Nordstrom department stores. Nordstrom has become a bit of a business legend with its no-questions-asked return policy, which dictates that its customer service agents must accept any return, under any condition, for any reason—at full refund. As one piece of popular lore has it, a man once entered a

Nordstrom store with a brand-new set of automobile tires. When the customer service agent politely explained to the man that Nordstrom does not, and never has, sold automobile tires, the man just gruffly pointed to a sign explaining Nordstrom's return policy, which technically didn't state that the product had to have been purchased at a Nordstrom! Knowing that, above all else, accountability to customers was core to the Nordstrom brand, the agent accepted the tires and provided a full refund—at a price she surely had to make up.

On the other end of the spectrum, to see the damage that can happen when transparency and accountability do *not* ripple out through employees—not just at the top of the company but at all rungs of the organization—one only has to look back as far as the aftermath of the 2007–2008 financial crisis, when it came to light that some of the world's largest investment banks were creating high-risk securities. As we now know, banks were making billions of dollars selling these securities to clients, all the while secretly betting big bucks against them. When these client investments crashed through the floor, the banks walked away with a second windfall of profits. The ultimate result, of course, was one of the worst financial collapses in history. Imagine how things might have ended differently had the banks been transparent and fostered a culture of accountability that allowed everyone—from managers and executives all the way down to junior associates and traders—to approach superiors about the fact that they were in essence playing poker with their clients' money.

While not every lapse of transparency and accountability is going to result in trillion-dollar meltdowns, things like predatory pricing, bait-and-switch advertising, misreported hours on an invoice, or any number of other less-than-genuine business practices will surely catch up to you—and cost you serious profits—if allowed to go on long enough. As Warren Buffett once said, "It takes a lifetime to build a reputation, but only fifteen seconds to destroy it." Transparency and accountability don't just happen—they're deliberately ingrained in organizations through ethos and process. As with all the lessons in this book, the sooner they're adopted, the better off you'll be.

MISSION BRIEF

- Transparency breeds trust, and trust is critical when everything is on the line.
- Transparency and accountability are necessary both internally and externally, in order to build the loyalty and confidence of everyone who matters to the success of your company, be they employees, customers, donors, or the general public.
- Use social media to tell your story and shed light on everything going on in your organization; it's a revolutionary tool—use it!
- Imagine you have an Eye of God holding you accountable for your every move—use it to conduct yourself in the right way in business as well as in your personal life.

- In a high-stakes business where you never know where or when the next challenge will arise, good results today are only half the battle—to sustain success in the long run, you must hold yourself and everyone on your team accountable for methodology as well.
- A little friendly competition within the organization is a great way to motivate teams while fostering accountability.
- Transparency and accountability ripple outward from the leader, through the organization, until they touch the consumer—at that point you've succeeded.

ANALYZE

It's not what you look at that matters,
it's what you see.
—HENRY DAVID THOREAU

In the above quote, famed nineteenth-century author Henry David Thoreau cleverly immortalizes a paradox that consistently plagues leaders, whether in the military or in business, your personal life or your weekly poker game. Being aware of opportunities, problems, and threats is only half the battle—that is simply ingesting information. How can we take this one step further and turn that information into something actionable? How can we not just look, but rather *see?*

The applications for leaders in high-stakes situations are plenty. First, we have to know where to look—that doesn't happen by accident. Learning how to capitalize on different tools and methods of observation—and understanding the importance of them—is the first critical step. Once observed, these data points then must be prioritized and processed—they must be turned into an actionable intelligence picture.

Ask yourself this question: Do you truly see what you're looking at? As an old English proverb states, "There's none so blind as those who won't see."

LESSON 4

Find and Prioritize Your Targets

With beads of sweat pooling on my brow, I pulled my eyes away from the spotting scope and looked down at the mat I was laying on. Reaching up, I used the back of my hand to wipe the sweat away and then gently rubbed my tired eyes. I'd been lying flat on the baking asphalt of a nondescript road in the middle of Camp Pendleton, the Marine Corps base in Southern California that was home to the Scout Sniper School. The heat was radiating upward, making it difficult to concentrate. Looking out of the corner of my eyes to the left and right, I could see a dozen men on either side, each one just as hot and miserable. "Five minutes, you pigs!" the instructor yelled.

Glancing down at my paper, I quickly panicked. I had only discovered eight of the ten objects that were skillfully hidden by the instructors in the massive field in front of me; and I was only half sure about two of those eight. I needed to find the other two objects before time was up or I could potentially fail the observation exercise—one of the critical "field tests" in Sniper School, and one of the most mentally grueling. It was designed to teach snipers the technical skill of identifying visual anomalies in the landscape—what doesn't belong or is unnatural—as well as the strategic methods of observation: how to know where to look. "Who's going to fail? Which one of you do I get to send home today?" the instructor taunted, pacing back and forth down the long line of our sprawled-out boots.

Putting my eyes back up to the spotting scope, I started to control my breathing, focusing on bringing in oxygen so that my brain would function at its highest capacity. I scanned the field in deliberate grid-squares from right to left, looking for abnormalities. *Remember the indicators,* I thought. *Shine, Outline, and Contrast to background.* Over the previous weeks I had trained my eyes to observe these indicators, each of which are generally characteristics of man-made objects—like an enemy rifle. I paused the scope on a bush two hundred yards away that had caught my attention earlier—something just wasn't right. I repeated the indicators in my head, looking for any hint that there was a foreign object hidden away in the thick branches of the bush. Reaching up, I dialed the focus ring in and out, changing the depth of view. Finally, I saw it. The slightest glancing ray of sunlight, reflected off the tinted glass lens of a pair of "enemy" binoculars. Earlier I must have seen the circular outline of the lens, an abnormally perfect shape in a randomly thorny bush. Obviously it had not been enough to spot the binoculars, but, forty-five minutes later, the sunlight was just now striking the surface and reflecting ever so slightly. Quickly I removed my eyes from the scope and scribbled down on my worksheet a description of the object and its place on the "battlefield."

"Two minutes! Two minutes until I put my boot in someone's ass and send them back to their unit a failure that dared waste my time!"

I put my eyes back up to the scope and shifted my focus to the left. Immediately, my gaze fell upon an object I had observed earlier, a pineapple grenade resting amid a pile of dark rocks about one hundred and fifty yards away. Within only a few seconds my heart sank. The grenade, it turns out, was in fact just another rock, gnarled and shaped like the iconic explosive. I cursed myself under my breath and scratched the object off my list. I was back down to eight objects.

"You stupid pigs probably don't even know how close you are to being sent home. So close. So damn close!" The instructor laughed, taking great joy as the seconds ticked down and the sniper students panicked. "So close!"

Suddenly I realized it was a hint. *There's a danger-close target!* I thought, pulling my face away from the scope and instead shielding my eyes from the sun with both hands. My eyes quickly moved along the terrain immediately in front of me, moving from right to left along the edge of the road. Not seeing anything, I scooted back and placed my chin on the hot asphalt, getting as low to the deck as possible. Repeating the scan, my eyes caught the faintest anomaly—a slight protrusion above the edge of the road's outline. It was only eight feet away, but I couldn't quite make out what it was. A blade of grass? Or perhaps a single round of rifle ammunition standing vertically? I grabbed a pair of binoculars from my side and brought them to my eyes. Smiling, I placed them back down and picked up my pencil, sloppily sketching a single rifle round onto my worksheet. Nine out of ten complete.

"Time! Pencils down and eyes off the glass! Hand your worksheets into the center, now!"

REMEMBERING YOUR INDICATORS

As I mentioned earlier, a Marine sniper's job is much more than simply shooting long distances. An enormous portion of their job involves surveillance and observation, a skill that was put to the test time and again in exercises like the one just described, and put into practice on the battlefields of Afghanistan. Observation is a powerful skill that every good Marine must cultivate; after all, spotting an enemy attacker or explosive just a millisecond too late can mean the difference between life and death.

In today's highly volatile business world, observation is a crucial skill for a leader as well. It is what allows us to identify both threats and opportunities, whether internal or external, obvious or subtle. It may not be life or death, but the ability to spot an encroaching product or competitor, an unhinged coworker, or a festering problem at the earliest possible moment can mean the difference between success and failure. Likewise, success often rests on the ability to identify an untapped need or market, a high-potential talent, or an area for personal career advancement before anyone else. In business, as in battle, equally important as spotting these "targets" is prioritizing the multiple targets discovered—ranking opportunities or threats in a prioritized manner, taking into account impact, proximity, and probability.

In today's business world, where the terrain is rapidly shifting and the "enemy" often appears unannounced, out of nowhere, leaders must be highly attuned to a myriad of things—their employees, their competitors, their customers or clients, government regulation and legislation, the economy, technology, and even themselves (just to name a few!). With so many areas of observation, how can a leader possibly be attuned to them all? The hard truth is that you can't. However, what you can do is hone your observational skills by understanding some key concepts.

Establish a Baseline

One of the first orders of business for a sniper team on a surveillance mission is to establish the baseline. The baseline is the natural harmony of any ecosystem; in a war zone it could include sights, sounds, smells, schedules, pace of life, nature of human interaction, etc. For example, when I was on tour in Afghanistan, our team was sent to an Afghan Army outpost for a week to conduct some joint operations with Afghan troops. Over the first two days we observed a pattern of life outside the base that went like this: The sun rose, women emerged from compounds to milk the livestock, the men began milling about in huddled groups smoking cigarettes, later children would walk toward the main road to attend school, and so on. On the third or fourth day, however, we noticed that the women were not leaving the compounds to milk the livestock as usual, and the men were huddled in one large group, rather than a few smaller ones. When the children never emerged to head to school we knew something was amiss. Quietly we roused the other members of the team, and all six manned the compound wall in full gear. Sure enough, within minutes the compound was under attack. Luckily, because we'd been attuned to the baseline in the area, we anticipated the assault and were prepared.

Determining the baseline of human behavior was equally critical when Team Rubicon rolled into Port-au-Prince. As chaotic as that situation was, knowing the local routines and customs that had become the norm in the wake of the disaster helped us determine if an area was particularly dangerous, and if so, what our options were to provide aid. For example, the norm in Haiti in the first weeks following the earthquake was for family units to be together at all times—fathers serving as providers and pro-tectors for their wives and children. Whole families trav-eled together, stood in lines together, sought help together. So, if our teams found that large groups of middle-aged men were breaking away from the women and children to gather and watch our movements, it would cause concern and force our team to evaluate whether they were at risk of being robbed for food, water, or medicine.

Establishing a baseline is critical for anyone, in any professional endeavor. Think of the trial lawyer. Naturally, any trial hinges on the jury, so establishing a jury's base-line behavior is paramount. Under normal circumstances, how do the people on the jury interact? What are their facial expressions? Is it unusual for them to nod their head? Take notes? In general, are they alert and attentive? Knowing these baseline measures not only helps a trial lawyer craft her language and tactics, it alerts her when the jury has a strong reaction—positive or negative—to something that's been said. Is her line of questioning resonating well with Juror Number 3, who appears to be a critical influencer in the box? What does it mean if Juror Number 4, who has been staring into space throughout a witness's testimony, starts furiously taking notes during the cross-examination? Being attuned to these subtle shifts in mood, body language, and behavior tells a lawyer what's working and what isn't, so she can course-correct.

Here is just one of many examples of the importance of baselines in business. Think of a restaurant entrepreneur, who has observed that one elderly customer comes in every Tuesday for lunch, and has for months. What baselines might this customer provide? Does the customer order the same thing every time? What is the size of the tip? How long does he stay? Does he interact with the waitstaff? Assume the customer has ordered the patty melt and left a big tip every day for the last five years, but suddenly begins ordering the BLT and not tipping. What does that mean? Has the service taken a nosedive? Is the new line-cook bad at making patty melts? Has the restaurant's supplier been sending contaminated beef?

The truth is you'll never know to ask those questions if you have not been deliberate in studying the baseline. On the sniper team we used to keep an observation log for just that purpose. In it, as you might imagine, we logged every observation made on the battlefield—every last one, big or small. Every car that drove past was logged by time, direction, color, and model. Every individual or group that entered the area of observation was noted by size, gender, makeup, age, activity, attire, and any other indicator we could think of. Only with this type of consistent observation can patterns be established, and only with an understanding of patterns can abnormalities be detected and acted upon.

With the rise of "big data" making the collection and analysis of baseline information easier and cheaper than ever, there is no reason why your observational efforts should be any less constant and consistent. Being constant means that you commit yourself and your organization to regular, deliberate collection methods—whether that is on a minute-by-minute, hourly, daily, or weekly basis. Think of accounting, in which consistency is one of the primary principles—report it the same way, every time, so that results can be measured against one another month by month, quarter by quarter, year by year.

What are some obvious sources of information needed to establish your baseline in virtually any type of business?

- Customer demographics
- Financial data
- Growth rates
- Social media metrics
- Employee, customer, and competitor behavior

In addition to these, there are other, less obvious areas of observation. For example, you may not think issues like geopolitics affect your business, but you may be making a terrible mistake. Any leader, particularly an entrepreneur venturing into new waters, or anyone in a volatile or rapidly changing industry or field, should have their finger on the pulse of major new laws or regulatory shifts—like a new health care law or new patent restrictions or new allowances for startup funding—that are affecting their industry. Even broad cultural shifts, such as legalization of marijuana or gay marriage, can impact a wide array of businesses in unexpected ways. No matter your official role in the organization, you'll be well served to keep your eyes open to subtle shifts in the baseline, so that when big change happens—and it will—you'll be prepared.

Shine, Outlast, and Contrast to Background

Disturbances to the baseline don't have to be as obvious as the abrupt departure from the pattern of life that led to my unit being attacked in Afghanistan. On some missions our clue that something was amiss was as inauspicious as an absence of chirping birds; or, in one amazing case, an Afghan interpreter smelling spices in the market that were not common to the Helmand Valley, but were in fact native to Pakistani foreign fighters.

The story at the beginning of this chapter referred to three visual cues that indicate irregularities in nature: shine, outline, and contrast to background. In business, is your problem or threat going to shine in the sun, have straight contours when it's surrounded by broken outlines, or stand out as light gray in a green bush? Probably not! But these cues are just extreme examples of what every leader should be looking for at all times: abnormalities, things that disturb the natural order of things (i.e., the baseline).

Naturally, the extent to which a disturbance merits further investigation depends on the context; on the battlefield, rocks lined up alongside the road can be a sign of serious danger, whereas in an area that's been hit by a hurricane, a line of rocks isn't particularly dangerous or indicative. As a leader, it is your job to determine the abnormalities you are looking for. The first question a leader must ask him- or herself is, "Do I know what I'm looking for?" Is it something specific—something with defined characteristics and metrics, perhaps a drop in customer retention, or a swing in operating costs, or even something as seemingly insignificant as fewer cars in the employee parking lot—that would indicate a notable deviation from baseline conditions? Or is it more a gut feeling, perhaps that a client is unhappy or a valued team member is preparing to defect to the competition, or that internal strife is brewing on the board of directors? When you know the parameters of what you're seeking, you can set up filters that reduce the "noise" and only tell you what may be relevant.

Often, the process of filtering information can be delegated or automated. Imagine that you're an investment banker looking for new opportunities—immediately you'll have some filters preestablished for you as dictated by the strategy set forth by the firm: deal size, industry, EBITDA thresholds, P/E ratios, etc. Based on these, you can automate your influx of information about potential deals to return only a subset from the larger market. In this example, not all of these deals will turn out to be winners, and only vast industry knowledge, research, and experience can help you tell the difference. Perhaps you've found that companies led by founder-CEOs tend to return higher value in acquisition deals. Or that companies led by founders with tech backgrounds (computer science engineers, for example), return an even higher payout because their lack of business expertise provides an even riper opportunity to improve core numbers. It's important to establish structured filters whenever possible, and luckily, thanks to the emergence of "big data," leaders and organizations now have the ability to mine millions of data sets to uncover observations that would not have been possible even ten years ago.

Of course, filters are not a substitute for human observation—merely a tool to reduce the volume of information humans have to wade through in order to identify opportunities or threats. Think back to the story of the field observation exercise. Imagine for a moment that the instructors had told us at the beginning of the exercise that an RPG (rocket propelled grenade) was hidden out in the field. Knowing this, we could reduce the area of observation from the entire field to just those places on the field capable of hiding an object the size of an RPG. Or further still, we could have set our mind to detect the distinct characteristics of an RPG: the straight lines of a cylindrical tube (straight lines are uncommon in nature), the conical shape of the exhaust outlet, the tapered edge of the rocket itself, the distinct drab olive-colored body, or the potential for shine where the paint had chipped off. By setting our mind to filter outlines, shapes, and contrasts that matched these descriptions, we would have been able to detect potential hiding spots for the sought-after object. We then would have been able to more efficiently investigate only high-potential spots first, saving time and effort.

Change Your Perspective

Even the best Marines can suffer from fatigue when forced to observe the same minefield, the same terrain, the same conditions for days on end. Likewise, even the best leaders can suffer from observation fatigue when looking at the same scene, data set, or industry environment over and over. It is natural that after extended periods of time, extreme familiarity numbs our minds and our senses, making it difficult to pick up on abnormalities and disruptions. In order to avoid this, it is critical for leaders to constantly change perspectives through any combination of a few methods—external, literal, figurative, and temporal.

EXTERNAL

External perspective is exactly what it sounds like—getting advice or guidance from outside the problem (though not necessarily outside the organization). Sometimes we are so close to—or so biased about—a problem that we are incapable of seeing it clearly. This situation is particularly common in start-ups when founders are involved. Founders, me included, are often so passionate about their endeavor that they can only see things for how they should be, not how they really are. In our minds, the vision and strategy are so clear and sound that they couldn't possibly have any flaws—but how often we find ourselves wrong! At Team Rubicon, William and I serve as each other's external perspective. Because we often find ourselves pitted against one another on opposite sides of strategy, and sometimes even on vision, we know we'll never settle into groupthink as we observe the landscape surrounding our organization. What I might glaze over as the norm will raise alarm bells for William, and vice versa. As a result, I'd recommend any small organization have a diverse core leadership team, with many different perspectives, ideals, and technical and interpersonal skills represented. Always invite the contrarian into the conversation.

External perspective is also critical in large organizations, where a problem can be so widespread that no single leader can observe enough from all the various areas (or, in business jargon, *verticals*) within the organization to stitch together the bigger-picture issues or opportunities. In cases such as this, you'll often see large corporations bring in external consulting firms. Many people are opinionated about consultants, with some claiming they're godsends and others disparaging them as a waste of money. After all, why pay high-priced consultants to come in and observe your problems—can't you do that yourself? It's that type of prideful thinking that can get organizations into trouble. At their core, consultants are observers first, problem solvers second. But if you are in the "consultants are a waste of money" camp, your organization, whether large or small, can achieve a similar result by creating a strong board of directors. A strong, active, and diverse board, with genuine oversight and objectivity, can provide fresh eyes, ears, and perspectives to uncover threats and opportunities that the bleary-eyed leaders might miss.

Getting a fresh perspective doesn't have to involve this much effort. Ever found yourself staring at the same Excel spreadsheet or Word document for hours, unable to track down the single error—or insight—that is staring you right in the face? How long must we suffer before we simply yell at the associate down the hall to come and have a look? You'll be shocked how often that problem that vexes you is painfully easy for someone else—even if they report to you.

LITERAL

Remember the story about the observation drill I told at the beginning of this chapter? Recall that as the final minutes were counting down, I began looking for objects that were very close to me, but that after a few frantic seconds of not seeing anything I changed my perspective by lowering my eyes ten inches to ground level—literally changing my perspective. You might be wondering why ten inches would make a difference. Well, after moving my eyes down to the ground I was at the proper angle to see a rifle round poking up above the road, silhouetted against the sky, whereas when I had had my chin ten inches higher it was invisible because its outline blended in with the field behind it. That subtle shift changed everything, and revealed what was before invisible.

Similarly, in business, we can change perspective by literally shifting where we, as leaders, place ourselves. At Team Rubicon my role has continued to morph as the organization grows. With every member added, every hire made, every budget increase, my role moves further and further away from the on-the-ground action. On the first mission in Haiti I was the team leader, but because the team was so small I spent much less time leading than I did tending to horrific wounds from the earthquake. Compare that to Hurricane Sandy, three years and fifteen thousand volunteers later, during which I didn't get to the "front line" until nearly ten days after the storm made landfall. During those ten days I was with our headquarters element coordinating strategy, organizing logistics, and drumming up support from corporate and individual donors to finance the operation. Luckily we had incredible team leaders who were confident, competent, and empowered to achieve incredible things within that first week after the storm. It was a much different perspective than normal for me, but the size and scope of the operation dictated that it was a necessity. What will always remain important is that I, as a leader, recognize the limitations of this perspective shift—and no longer assume that I have as strong a pulse with the front lines.

For example, after the devastating Moore, Oklahoma, tornadoes, we launched an enormous operation that would become our largest and most successful ever. The tornadoes struck while I was speaking at a conference in London, and by the time I'd returned to our headquarters in Los Angeles, the operation was well underway. And so I helped manage operations remotely for about a week before heading down to Oklahoma to observe our leaders on the ground. While on the ground close to the action—a literally different perspective from my headquarters role—I observed a number of things that proved critical to Team

Rubicon's future. Perhaps most important, in reconnecting with the pulse of the core volunteer leadership, I learned that many of them were extremely frustrated with some cultural shifts that were happening within the organization. Because my perspective was generally distant from most volunteers, I wasn't able to adequately feel the pulse; but getting out on the ground took me back to the front lines, where I could sense this discontent. Understanding the importance of these observations, William and I set out to take drastic action and corrected the course we were on.

No matter what kind of business you're in or what your leadership role is, it's important to always change your perspective, in the literal sense. If you've outsourced production overseas, you should make it a habit to visit your manufacturing partners on site at least once per year. If you have been tasked with turning around an underperforming division at a large company, it would be wise to spend a week in the manager's office of each department for the first quarter, in order to see issues through their eyes. If you own your own retail business and think you know how your competition is doing, when was the last time you walked into their store and took the competition for a spin? Oh, and if you happen to run a nationwide disaster response nonprofit, get your ass to the front lines and drink beer with the troops—you might be surprised at what you hear.

FIGURATIVE

"Turn the chessboard around." Many people have heard this phrase, but few know how to put it into practice as well as the military. In the military, however, we call it *turn-*

ing the map around. One of the first things that a military leader does when fortifying his position is look at the map from the enemy's perspective. If I were the enemy, we ask, how would I attack my current location? It's not a simple discussion, either. Good military leaders will bring in their junior leaders and have an all-out offensive strategy session against their own defensive position—and then put together a plan to defend against it.

The lesson here is that observation isn't just about shifting your literal perspective, it's about shifting your internal one as well. Sometimes, in order to accomplish this type of introspection, you have to shift your internal mindset to that of the competition. Let's say you are building a company that is introducing a product into a market with an entrenched competitor—let's say a sports drink in Gatorade's backyard. A shrewd leader would change her perspective and imagine that she is Gatorade's VP of marketing, charged with burying the young upstart before it gets off the ground. Knowing that the start-up doesn't have the funds to wage a toe-to-toe battle on the marketing front, you might conduct a study that shows young adults (your most sought-after market) are heavily influenced by celebrity endorsement. Then, with that knowledge, you might go out and sign Johnny Football to a multiyear marketing deal, and launch a campaign with Johnny saying he'd never trust his hydration to a product other than Gatorade.

Now flip the map back around to your actual situation. Thanks to that perspective shift, the actual you now realizes your greatest weakness is not your product, it's your war chest. You can't commission million-dollar studies or sign multimillion-dollar endorsements. What can you do? Perhaps you choose to wage guerilla warfare and pay smaller endorsement sums, not to pro athletes, but to popular amateur or minor league players, and distribute the unique videos not during the Super Bowl, but on YouTube. Or maybe you chip away at the validity of Gatorade's science, and frame it as a sugar-laden beverage contributing to a growing obesity epidemic—hardly the face of hardcore athletes.

This type of David vs. Goliath marketing strategy was played out brilliantly by a young, underfunded start-up called Dollar Shave Club. Dollar Shave Club has a business model whereby customers sign up for as low as a dollar a month to have brand-new, high-quality disposable razors shipped to them monthly. Lacking the marketing budget of larger players like Gillette, the Dollar Shave Club founder produced a series of hilarious and foul-language-fueled YouTube videos that quickly went viral. Now, Dollar Shave Club is steadily chipping away at the traditional razor power's market share. (To see why, do yourself a favor—put this book down and go watch a couple of their videos. They're worth a laugh or two, and will colorfully shed light on this section.)

The lesson is that turning around the map and observing your own position through the eyes of the competition, and doing it collaboratively and creatively, is an incredibly useful exercise that can breed constructive criticism and reveal unseen weaknesses and opportunities.

TEMPORAL

Time can be a powerful, albeit dangerous, variable in business. This is true today more than ever, when industries and markets and technologies are evolving at lightning speed. And as these things change with time, the manner in which we observe them also changes. So as you look for targets in your business context, always consider allowing time to pass to see whether your observations change. Perhaps the anomaly you discovered will prove to just be a onetime event, and not indicative of something warranting broader concern. Or perhaps you'll see things differently due to your own personal growth (new knowledge and understanding of an issue, perhaps), the introduction of new information, or external influence (remember the setting sun reflecting off the glass of the binoculars in the opening story). Sometimes the simple passage of time can lend us a much-needed shift in perspective.

Imagine this: An upstart competitor flames you on the internet with false accusations that your product is harmful to [insert: *babies, kittens,* or *puppies*]. Having previously observed the reactionary nature of your customer base, you immediately believe that this is going to devastate sales if left unaddressed and uncorrected. However, before issuing a knee-jerk public rebuttal, potentially drawing more (unnecessary) attention to the issue, you wait to see if there will be any initial outcry. If not, you can perhaps address the claim via less conspicuous means.

Of course, there is danger in this approach. The danger is getting stuck in a mindset of inaction; of believing that things will get better with time, and that you don't have to do anything. The result of this attitude is either complacency or a false sense of hope, and both are killers. So while sometimes it's prudent to wait to see if your perspective changes over time, take care not to wait too long, particularly in situations that are fast moving and time sensitive—like the timing of an IPO, for example—where hesitation could end up costing you or your company substantial money or opportunity.

PRIORITIZE YOUR TARGETS

In football, a blitzer coming through the center of the line always becomes the priority block, because he has the shortest path to the quarterback. In disaster medicine, patients are triaged by priority: critical, urgent, priority, low priority, and expectant. Critical patients can die within the hour if untreated; expectant patients *will* die within the hour, regardless of care. Expectant patients—although the most severely wounded—are not treated. It is a tough decision to make; however, any time and resources expended, beyond those which quickly reduce their pain and suffering, are time and resources taken away from patients that have a chance of survival.

The system for prioritizing targets I reference most often, however, comes from my military training as a sniper. Snipers often insert themselves behind enemy lines in advance of a major battle, in a concealed position that offers a broad perspective of the battlefield so they can observe and report timely and critical information to commanders, as well as take precision shots at selected targets. Marine snipers have a very specific target priority list ingrained in them throughout training; and as important as memorizing the list is knowing why the list is ordered that way, and what effect it will have on the battlefield. At the top are enemy snipers, since they are often the most effective and demoralizing enemy soldiers on the battlefield. Next are enemy officers, since they direct the battle and issue orders. Then come radio operators (to cut lines of communication and create confusion) and machine gunners (to prevent death in large numbers from their rapid rates of fire). Last (with a few more in between) are common riflemen. The single caveat to all this is the "danger-close target," or plainly, any enemy, regardless of rank or function, who presents himself in front of you within fifty yards and therefore takes priority over all other targets. At that range any enemy, regardless of skill, is a mortal danger.

How to translate this lesson to the business world—and life in general—is obvious. In any given high-stakes situation, a large variety of problems—and opportunities—are going to present themselves. But they will not all be equal in importance—far from it. Effective leaders understand this, and hold their fire on the low-priority targets so they can focus on hitting the high-priority ones. These leaders understand that every expenditure—whether capital invested, hours logged, or employee hired—must have maximal impact. The ability to channel these resources to the most critical threats—and the highest potential opportunities—is a skill that's often overlooked, but can be cultivated with awareness, practice, and consistent execution.

As I've stated, on the battlefield the top-priority target is enemy snipers—they're hidden, and with a single shot can demoralize or destroy a unit. Similarly, in business, the highest-priority targets are the threats facing your company that you know are out there, but that you cannot readily see. Is your competitor pouring money into research and development? You had better be prepared for a new product launch that is going to potentially shatter your market share. Do you have a huge, gaping hole in insurance coverage that, if discovered through an accident rather than an audit, is going to bankrupt your company? Luckily, a healthy dose of paranoia is usually all that's necessary to discover and defend against these hidden and top-priority threats.

What about another critical priority: the danger-close target? Remember, anything on the battlefield that presents itself within fifty yards is considered danger-close, and takes priority. In the business sense, we'll define "close" as either in actual physical proximity (someone on your team, perhaps) or in time (suddenly, while working on addressing a critical concern with a three-month horizon, a critical issue that must be resolved within three weeks is identified). Often, leaders are so concerned with a threat looming on the horizon that they lose sight of seemingly innocuous problems or threats brewing under their very noses. Just remember to keep in mind that the seemingly harmless issue that you planned on taking care of when time permitted might suddenly develop into a danger-close target that will have to be dealt with immediately.

The problem leaders often have is that when the pressure is on—when things become crazy, or when failure seems a possibility—it can be tempting to focus on identifying and solving the easy problems. After all, the low-priority targets are often the easiest ones to hit; and even if the group as a whole fails, if I can point to a series of individual successes, no matter how inconsequential, I can feel good that I didn't contribute to the defeat. What a terrible mindset!

Another mistake we often see, when the stakes are high, is teams or individuals addressing problems or opportunities simply in the order they present themselves. This is equally absurd! Imagine if, when Team Rubicon went to Haiti, we told the Haitians simply to get in a line to seek medical attention, and we'd treat them as they came to the front. We would have had amputations sitting fifty-people-deep while we treated bumps and scrapes!

Step Above the Fray

So what's the best way to prevent this poor prioritization of targets in business? Ensure that as a leader you stay above the fray. By this I mean leaders need to lead, not execute. In high-stakes situations in particular, it's the leader's job to observe broadly across the entire threat and opportunity landscape, deftly redirecting resources and efforts to address the most critical problems and capitalize on the highest potential opportunities as they arise. Focusing on the nitty-gritty of execution can distract from these crucial responsibilities. It's often difficult for leaders to do this; for many leaders, their true passion is in the execution (and it was probably their skill at execution that got them promoted to the leadership role in the first place). Think of the VP at the trading firm who loves nothing more than to buy and sell tens of millions of dollars in securities every hour, winning or losing with every trade—but now finds himself in an endless loop of management responsibilities and board meetings. Or the firefighter who suddenly makes captain, and is devastated that he'll no longer be the first man into the burning building. Or the five-star chef turned restaurant entrepreneur who has to force himself reluctantly out of the kitchen to deal with diners, suppliers, and investors.

The Marine Corps used to have an interesting trick to ensure their officers weren't directly engaging in combat themselves, but rather "managing" their men by moving up and down the skirmish line directing fields of fire and repositioning defenses. They didn't issue officers rifles! After all, it's pretty hard (and stupid) to insert yourself into the battle if you don't have an adequate weapon (the Marines did issue officers pistols as a self-defense weapon, but that's hardly anything you want to rely on in combat). That policy has changed in recent years, but the thought process was spot-on. Leaders—and as we've seen, the Marine Corps knows a thing or two about leadership—win battles by prioritizing and exploiting opportunities presented by the enemy, not by putting themselves into the line of fire.

Admittedly, in business, staying off the front lines is often easier said than done, especially in resource-starved start-ups. There's a reason entrepreneurs joke that CEO stands for Chief Everything Officer—I've been there at Team Rubicon. In our early days, William and I were knee-deep in handling day-to-day tasks and issues, and had to convene in the evenings and on weekends to have even a chance to discuss high-level strategy and analysis. But the fact is, tempting as it can be to stay involved in the day-to-day operations, once you've put your trusted teams in place, and trained them with the skills they need, as a leader, your time and efforts are better spent prioritizing targets, rather than shooting at them. So while putting in your time and knowing all the functions of your business is important, do yourself and your organization a favor and, as soon as you're able, step above the fray.

Now, Prioritize

Every industry and every team function is so unique that it is challenging for me to provide broad-stroke guidance on how to prioritize threats and opportunities. It's very possible that you'll have multiple seemingly high-priority threats and opportunities at the same time. If this happens to you, congratulations, you can now be certain that what you do is high-stakes! What's important is, first, that you observe them; second, that you rank and analyze them; and finally, that you communicate and discuss that prioritization with your team.

So now that you've learned how to spot the targets, and rank them according to their priority, it's time to communicate that prioritization to the team. Hopefully you already understand the importance of discussing and communicating problems openly and transparently. So just remember that when these problems are the business equivalent of "enemy fire," it becomes even more important to make sure that each member of a team, and each team within an organization, knows which problems are important to solve immediately, and which can take a temporary backseat—and likewise, which opportunities are important to go after full-throttle, and which are lower-priority. Then let them put their nose to the grindstone and execute relentlessly with the confidence that you, as a leader, are competently and constantly observing and reprioritizing their targets—and communicating those priorities effectively.

MISSION BRIEF

- The first key to observation is to know your baseline; and establishing it requires a commitment to consistency.
- Seek anomalies in the baseline and evaluate them.
- Find anomalies by shifting your perspective: externally, literally, figuratively, or temporally.
- It is important for leaders to "stay above the fray" and let others do the figurative fighting.
- Prioritize your targets; always seek out the "snipers"—the hidden problems and opportunities behind enemy lines—and the "danger-close" targets—the critically dangerous problems that arise out of nowhere.
- It's your job to prioritize and communicate; it's your team's job to execute!

LESSON 5

Create Actionable Intelligence

"How high are the exterior walls?" a scruffily bearded man with a thick wad of chewing tobacco asked as he spit into a cup.

The woman at the head of the briefing table, upon which sat a to-scale replica of a nondescript building, responded, "Approximately three meters all the way around."

"Balcony wall?"

"A little over two meters."

Another man, thickly muscled and heavily tattooed forearms folded across his chest, cleared his throat and spoke. "Do the doors open inward or outward?"

"Outward."

"How thick are they and what material?"

"Don't know and don't know."

The man grunted at the response and pulled a tooth-pick out of his mouth. "Weapons?"

The woman hesitated briefly before answering, "We have not been able to confirm or deny the presence of weapons in the compound. We have to assume that the military-aged males will be armed with AK-47s, and we are operating under the assumption that all individuals, to include the women, will be wearing suicide vests"—she paused before continuing—"but the truth is, we simply don't know."

For the next fifteen minutes the woman answered questions from the Navy SEALs gathered around the table, until finally the last inquiry had been addressed. Stepping back from the table, she put her hands on her hips. "Gentlemen, I understand there might be some frustration at the lack of information, particularly that we cannot tell you with one hundred percent certainty that OBL is at this compound. But I will tell you this—there is not a doubt in my mind that the indicators point to his presence, and I will stake everything on that. We have enough information to put together a battle plan that I have no doubt you can execute, and if we pull this off, it might be the greatest military and intelligence community achievement in history."

I obviously wasn't at the initial intelligence briefing given to SEAL Team Six prior to the incredible operation that led to the death of Osama bin Laden, but I imagine that the question and answer portion went much like the above version I've imagined. Military operators, my former sniper teammates included, have an unquenchable thirst for information—wouldn't you if you were about to go kick in a door that potentially had suicide bombers on the other side? But what's important about the dialogue above is that it demonstrates that in high-stakes situations, no matter how much we might want answers to the questions we're asking, we don't always get them—whether in the board-room or on the battlefield, we don't always have all the information we want, and often not even the information we feel we need to make a "safe" decision.

In fact, I'd go so far as to say that the lack of timely and credible information is a hallmark of high-stakes situations in business. If you knew what a company's quarterly profits were going to be, investing heavily in it wouldn't be a risk. If you knew for sure that consumers were going to trample each other on Black Friday racing to buy your product, spending to manufacture and market it would be a no-brainer. If you could foresee that a scrappy start-up would come out of nowhere and steal away 30 percent of your market, you could prepare to pivot into a new customer segment. But the reality is, as mere mortals without the ability to see into the future, we rarely have this kind of information in advance. So as leaders, how can we make decisions and operate effectively in situations with incomplete information?

First, we must accept the reality of our information gap. Rather than wringing our hands and complaining about the lack of information, the best leaders are those who make the most of the information available. The best leaders are the ones who know that there's no sense in sitting around waiting for complete information to appear—because by the time it does, it will probably be too late to act. Instead, the best leaders and organizations are able to interpret and make sense of the information they have to create intelligence (which is very different, as we'll see in a minute, from mere facts or observation), then prioritize and seek the information they still need, and finally, move to act in a way that maximizes the chances for success.

In the last chapter we learned how to effectively observe the landscape around us and our organization, being sure to efficiently collect data points of information to help inform our decision making. However, each of these observations is merely an unrefined snippet of information and isn't the whole picture; it's merely one of many variables and pieces of information you need to factor in. In this chapter we'll look at how to construct as complete an intelligence picture as possible from these many disparate observations—and then translate that information into a plan for bold, decisive action.

INFORMATION VS. INTELLIGENCE

What are we talking about when we talk about information? Information is simply the individual segments of raw data and observations collected to help address a situation. Information is critical; however, information in its raw form is insufficient for making good strategic and tactical decisions. In order to effectively lead organizations in fluid and uncertain situations, leaders must work to transform information into *intelligence*. Intelligence is what is produced when trained experts (intelligence analysts in the military; operational planners in disaster response; senior executives and boards of directors in business) verify the information's validity, extract what is most relevant, extrapolate that data and draw correlations and connections, and finally synthesize that information into choices and probable impacts.

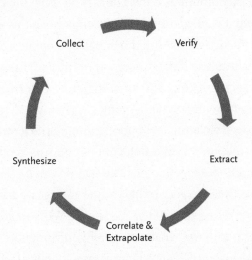

To help illustrate this cycle, I'll use the situation we found ourselves in prior to leaving for Port-au-Prince immediately after the 2010 earthquake. First, bear in mind that prior to the earthquake striking, Team Rubicon did not exist. In fact, William and I only knew each other through mutual friends, and had never met in person. So a formal information collection and intelligence generation mechanism did not exist; it was only the experience gained while planning high-stakes operations in the Marine Corps that allowed us to rapidly construct a complete picture based on many disparate sources of incomplete data (it also helped that William was a well-trained counterintelligence Marine).

Perhaps the most critical intelligence picture needed

after the Haiti earthquake was of the security and stability situation on the ground. After all, this single factor—how safe it was for responders on the ground—had the potential to impact hundreds of decisions, and if the intelligence was wrong it would cost thousands of lives—either ours or those of the people we would be unable to help.

Initial information, gathered via traditional news outlets and social media platforms, indicated that there were widespread security issues—gangs hijacking aid convoys, gender-based violence, retribution killings, and looting. But this information was anecdotal at best, and, as is often the case in high-stakes situations, we had no way of verifying it—by the time we got on the ground to observe the situation for ourselves, it would be too late. So William and I had no choice but to use whatever sketchy information we had to generate an intelligence picture on which we could take action. I'll walk you through how we did that step by step.

COLLECT

The methods of observation you learned about in the last chapter are, in essence, methods of collecting information. What is important to emphasize is that these methods will only be effective within a culture that places an emphasis on them. Everyone within a dynamic organization or endeavor should be constant collectors of information— from the CEO down to the mail clerk. In order for this to work, it must be communicated that information collection is a priority, and that yours is a workplace in which open communication and contribution are not only accepted but expected.

This has been the case in every high-stakes environment I've ever been involved with. In the military, nearly half my job was collecting information on the battlefield in order for commanding officers to generate intelligence from it. Even during football games at Wisconsin, every player, from quarterback to second-string (where I spent most of my time . . .), was tasked by the coaches to collect pieces of information. In my case this most often meant observing what cues opposing linebackers were giving prior to blitzing the line of scrimmage; anything I noticed I instantly disseminated to my position coach and to the starting offensive linemen.

At Team Rubicon, information is everything. In the aftermath of the Haiti earthquake the twenty-four-hour news cycle had images of the chaos in Port-au-Prince on near constant repeat. Initial reports, as stated earlier, indicated widespread and unwarranted violence. Because it was the most readily available information, William and I digested all the television and online media available in order to gain as many perspectives as possible. But we knew this was not the complete picture (remember, crucial to being a good leader is knowing how much you *don't* know). So we tried turning to other sources: Twitter, our network of professional affiliations, and of course, individuals who lived near the crisis. First, William contacted a friend in the military's intelligence community, who was part of a task force responsible for generating intelligence in that part of the world. Much of what he said corroborated the media frenzy. We also contacted a member of the Jesuit community who was located within Haiti; his perspective was a bit different. Things, he said, were very chaotic, and the population was in anarchy; however, outright violence was not taking place—although the potential was there. Finally, we established filters on Twitter to search for key words contained in tweets coming out of Haiti, in order to try and glean information directly from Haitians on the ground. It was challenging, due to the language gap, but not impossible.

We certainly didn't have all the information we wanted, and the information we had was coming primarily from sources we didn't know whether we could necessarily trust. However, with more and more lives being lost on the ground due to contaminated water, dehydration, and lack of medical care, we didn't exactly have the luxury of waiting for a more complete picture to present itself. We'd have to take the information we'd gathered and use it to figure out the best intelligence picture we could generate.

VERIFY

Information is only useful if it's true. When the pressure is on, incorrect information, if assumed true and acted upon, can prove catastrophic—whether the situation is a devastating earthquake, a sudden drop in your business's cash flow, or a looming economic collapse. So the more you have on the line, the more critical, albeit difficult, it is to verify inbound information. As Ronald Reagan famously said, "Trust, but verify."

There are numerous things to consider when verifying information; here are some of the most important:

Source: Where is the information coming from? Is the person or organization reputable? Have you relied on this source of information in the past? With what outcome? Just as important as the source are the source's motives. Does he or she have something to gain or lose based off the action you take according to the information provided? We took this cautious approach in assessing the reliability of the testimony coming from a Jesuit brother who was on the ground in Haiti. Knowing that he had a strong incentive to sway our opinion of violence in order to convince us to launch the mission and come to help his school of Jesuit brothers, we had to be careful that he was not "coloring" the truth. Over the course of a few conversations we asked probing questions aimed at painting a clearer picture of what he was actually seeing on the ground. If he hadn't seen acts of violence, had he seen armed mobs? If he hadn't seen convoys attacked, was it because he hadn't left his compound? If violence was not a problem, why did he have two armed Haitians at his gate at all times?

Evidence: You'd be shocked how often people refuse to let the facts get in the way of a good story. When someone makes a claim, always ask for evidence, even if that source is one you would consider reputable. If you're a business leader, you likely base many of your decisions off your financial books—when was the last time you had those books audited? I can't count the number of times I've heard stories of business owners getting embezzled and going bankrupt due to trusting an employee. To do anything but verify your information through evidence is simply laziness—and if you are a leader in a high-pressure situation, the last thing you can be is lazy.

Multiple sources: Has this information come to you

from multiple, unrelated sources? It is hard to ignore the same claim presented by people holding different perspectives.

Sniff Test: Don't underestimate the value of the good ol' common-sense test. Does the information seem plausible? Does it make sense? Often we find ourselves relying on information that flies in the face of reason. If it seems too far-fetched to be true, there's a good chance it is. Be careful though, because the reverse is true also; just because something "smells right" doesn't necessarily mean that it is. Don't fall into the trap of confusing familiarity with common sense.

Through the process of verification, information can be placed into one of three buckets: Confirmed, Denied, or Unverified. The first two are of course obvious: Information can be either true or false. The third, while seemingly as obvious, is actually the most difficult to consistently get accurate. We have a human tendency to want information to be proven either true or false; ambiguity and uncertainty cause us profound discomfort. In our desire to verify a piece of information, one way or another, we often find ourselves subconsciously skewing the evidence, and this can be very dangerous. So not only must we remain entirely impartial during the verification process, we must continuously remind ourselves that having information remain in the Unverified column is okay, because chances are that at some point in the intelligence cycle, new information may arise that helps confirm or deny its veracity.

When deciding whether or not to deploy our team to Haiti right after the earthquake, William and I had to be

very careful to remain impartial and not let our preconceived notions get in the way of verifying the incoming
information. Since I was already inclined to go to Port-au-
Prince to help, I was hoping that the information about
widespread violence was being overstated and sensationalized by the media. Knowing I had this existing bias, William and I took steps to draw conclusions independently
and compare notes. Did we ever collect enough evidence
to deny the veracity of the news media claims? No. But the
process did allow us to place claims of widespread violence
in the Unverified column; and our ability to confirm other
critical pieces of intelligence—availability of fresh water,
for instance—created the opportunity to make a "go" decision despite our inability to confirm or deny the violence.
Simply knowing what we didn't know proved invaluable
when it came time to make a decision and take action.

EXTRACT

Extraction of information is all about relevance. In our hy-
perconnected world, it is easy to become overwhelmed by
massive amounts of information. Too often we see organizations and leaders get bogged down by the "noise," or
facts that have little to do with the situation at hand. Effective leadership is about filtering through all this noise and
extracting that which is most relevant. We must be careful, however, not to discard information initially deemed
irrelevant. As situations evolve, the relevance of different
pieces of information will change (as may their accuracy).

Here, once again, it becomes important to take into
account the information's source. In the case of post-

earthquake Haiti, there were a few pieces of information regarding organizational movements on the ground that we extracted and paid specific attention to. First was the fact that the US military had announced that a Marine Expeditionary Unit (MEU) and a unit from the 101st Army Airborne were en route to the island to help provide security support. This news neither confirmed nor denied whether there was mass violence, but the MEU certainly had the ability to mitigate whatever violence may have been taking place. The second piece of information we paid careful attention to was reports from Doctors Without Borders—a French medical aid organization known for being willing to go anywhere under any circumstances—which indicated a "permissive" environment; in other words, the chaos and violence had not gotten so bad as to prevent the free movement and work of relief organizations. Honing in on the situation reports from a credible, on-the-ground source like Doctors Without Borders allowed us to largely tune out other, potentially sensationalized reports from organizations and agencies perhaps not as familiar with situations like the one presented in Port-au-Prince.

Another type of information you should pay special attention to is anything that seems unusual or outside the norm—in other words, the outliers. Imagine, for example, you work for a major retailer and are leading an effort to reconfigure store layouts in order to increase profit margins. The problem is, you have thousands of data sets from hundreds of existing stores. How do you parse them all? Out of this mountain of data, you should first identify your outliers—which stores have yielded consistently above- and below-average returns? Which stores have demonstrated a sharp increase in performance along your identified key performance indicators? Once the outliers have been identified, you can focus on the circumstances surrounding just those cases that will provide the most useful information.

In a perfect world we could staff up our business intelligence units to evaluate every scenario and data point, but in reality we must be able to extract that which is most relevant and make decisions quickly, sometimes relying on only a handful of key advisors.

EXTRAPOLATE AND CORRELATE

Once we've verified the veracity of information and selected that which is most relevant, we can begin to move into the real analysis of the information to create real, *actionable* intelligence. This can be achieved in one of two ways: through extrapolation or correlation.

Extrapolating information means determining which bits of information can be generalized and assumed true across multiple scenarios. In the case of the SEAL Team Six mission to kill or capture Osama bin Laden, for example, it is well known that most patriarchs in Pakistan own an AK-47, and they are commonplace in homes—terrorist cells or otherwise. It would have been safe to extrapolate this information and assume that every male in that Abbottabad compound was armed, at minimum, with an AK-47. This would then of course have informed the tactics devised in assaulting the compound.

Correlating information is the process of identifying

and drawing the connections between seemingly independent data points. Truth be told, outside of utilizing powerful software to analyze large data sets, correlating disparate
information is as much art as it is science. The question
a leader must ask is, "How do the data points I have presented before me interact with one another? Which influence which?" To truly get the most out of this process, one
must assemble a team that can think critically, communicate effectively, and consider outside-the-box hypotheses.
This team must be allowed to propose radical correlations
between data points and discuss them in a constructive
manner. In order to make this process as effective as possible and avoid groupthink, it's a good idea to designate
someone to play the role of contrarian. The contrarian's job
is to challenge assumptions and hypotheses relentlessly
(but not negatively). They ensure that nothing is taken at
face value. Sometimes you have to explore the craziest,
most "out there" hypotheses before you can begin to find
the ones that are truly sound.

Leading up to our departure for Port-au-Prince, for example, William and I worked to group our data points into
two sets of categories: those that increased (or decreased)
the probability of violence, and those that increased (or
decreased) the severity of violence. We then began to extrapolate and figuratively connect the dots to correlate information and test assumptions.

In the first set of categories, information that either increased or decreased the chance of violence, there was the
statement (unverified) by our Jesuit contact on the ground
that violence was not presently an issue. We forced ourselves

to verify this statement's truth, due to nearly two decades of human rights reports stating that despite US weapons embargoes in Haiti, police corruption and gang violence were constant problems—even before the earthquake. So we looked at two other correlating factors that may have *seemed* not to be related, but in fact were: the severity of the earthquake itself, and the tropical climate. First, the earthquake—images from Port-au-Prince showed near total destruction, and a working assumption that we made was that, by and large, if a Haitian didn't have it on their person at the time of the earthquake, any possession they owned was buried under a few tons of rubble. Meaning that unless they'd had their firearm on them when the quake struck, they more than likely couldn't get to it now. Second, thanks to our respective military trainings, we knew that the tropical humidity could make proper weapons maintenance (keeping them rust-free and operational) difficult, particularly considering the lack of weapons training available in Haiti. These facts, correlated with the lack of footage or photos of openly brandished firearms across the major TV networks, gave us confidence that the probability of violence was reduced (but certainly not eliminated).

From these probability insights we extrapolated to create a number of assumptions about the potential severity of the violence. We hypothesized that even the most hardened criminal elements, if they had been lucky enough to survive, would still be in a state of shock, and concerned first and foremost with stabilizing their families—rather than capitalizing on an opportunity to take organized criminal or violent action. Additionally, even if any single gang member had survived, that gang member's criminal infrastructure was diminished, as there was a high likelihood that his chain of command and ability to communicate were severed. However, we also knew that this window of "shock" would eventually close. Plus, knowing that the Marines and Army were en route fortunately gave us confidence that law and order would at least be restored on some level quickly, and that the *severity* of widespread violence, like a city-wide riot, was reduced. And in the end these hypotheses became key factors in our decision to assume the risk and deploy.

Obviously this is a very simplified breakdown of the extrapolation and correlation process, but the important takeaway is this—the process requires multiple people engaged in open dialogue, constantly proposing ideas, challenging assumptions, and trying to make connections that don't seem immediately obvious. As you move through the process of turning information into intelligence, I caution you from doing it in a vacuum. Instead, involve a team of trusted coworkers, taking particular effort to avoid yes-men and to add contrarian thinkers. Engage them in thoughtful discussion and, as the leader, allow everyone to challenge your own assumptions without fear of reprisal.

SYNTHESIZE

So now what? You collected, verified, extracted, extrapolated, and correlated, but have you created actionable intelligence? If you have come to a point where you are prepared to make a decision, then yes.

This final step—synthesizing information—involves

bringing all the elements together and painting a picture, in essence packaging it for dissemination and digestion. That picture might be one you want to see—favorable conditions that indicate a high chance of success; or one you don't want to see—unfavorable conditions that reduce that chance. Correlation and synthesis are similar, but think of correlation as connecting dots within similar data groups (i.e., the probability of violence), whereas synthesis interconnects completely different types of information to form a larger picture (i.e., how does the intersection of security, team composition, and water scarcity impact our decision to deploy to Port-au-Prince)?

Evaluate and Decide

So at this point you've completed the cycle and are staring at the intelligence picture. At this point, it doesn't matter whether the picture is good or bad, there's only one thing left to do—determine whether you have enough intel to make a decision. Be careful though; it's easy to fall victim to the trap of seeking perfect information. Leaders of fast-moving organizations must accept that they'll never have all the information they want—what's important is that you have an adequate intelligence picture for making a critical decision. If not, then you must immediately identify the critical pieces of information necessary to complete the picture—what the Marines call establishing Priority Information Requests (PIRs)—and set about having your team collect them. Naturally, the process of communicating and collecting PIRs should be happening throughout the cycle, but sometimes it's not until you see the full picture that you can determine which PIR is the single critical piece needed.

At some point a decision must be made—do you partner with the distributor? Do you fire the at-will employee you suspect of stealing proprietary information? Do you make a huge strategy pivot as your cash runway dwindles? Do you expand into a new market sector? The next chapter will be dedicated to the notion of the 80% Solution—a cultural mindset that helps you take decisive action in the face of imperfect intelligence and less-than-ideal conditions. Before that, there's one final note to keep in mind: In the world of high-stakes business, the intelligence cycle never ends.

Collection and Analysis Never End

What? Didn't I just say that you'll never have all the intelligence that you want, and that the sooner you can move from analysis to action the better? Yes! However, only a fool would move forward into action with blinders on. A constant loop of collection, analysis, and decision making must always be maintained to achieve success. In fact, it's even more crucial to keep creating intelligence *after* initial action has been taken, because facts and conditions will change and perspectives will shift, all working to create a completely new intelligence picture.

As these new information tidbits become available, they must be inserted into the intelligence cycle and utilized.

Naturally, the process of moving through the cycle gets faster and faster as you go through more iterations, so don't be intimidated with the idea of moving through it again. Think of the intelligence cycle as a slowly rotating storm system. It begins as a massive, undefined mass without much uniform direction or shape. But, slowly, as it moves through a series of rotations and begins to define itself, it become a taught, finely formed twister, spinning quickly and moving forward, changing directions as conditions and information change. New information inputs help refine assumptions made in the previous cycle, which more clearly defines the intelligence picture, which in turn refines the PIRs, which leads to iterative action, which leads to new information, and the cycle begins again. The good news is that you'll get better and more precise at collecting, verifying, extrapolating, and correlating information with every rotation, and soon moving through the cycle is natural and no longer cumbersome.

How did this play out in Haiti? William and I made the decision to deploy with an intelligence picture indicating violence was a possibility and, if met, potentially deadly (we did so knowing that our training would help us operate in a manner that would reduce the probability and severity of violence). Once on the ground, however, we realized that the reports *were* in fact inflated. Our teams did see a few unruly-looking citizens with firearms and sporadic police services, but the local populace was, for the most part, not as aggressive as we'd feared. After quickly extrapolating the new details we had before us, we pivoted and made the call to activate a team of doctors and nurses out of Chicago, and Team Rubicon more than doubled the size of its operations within days.

Truly innovative organizations and effective leaders thrive in situations that are in constant states of flux, because it allows them to rapidly iterate and adapt faster than the competition. However, in order for leaders and organizations to have this level of flexibility, they must have a clear and real-time intelligence picture.

MISSION BRIEF

- Information is simply the unprocessed data points collected through observation; intelligence is what is produced when information is verified, extracted, correlated, extrapolated, and synthesized into something actionable.
- To verify information, be sure to consider the source, number of sources, and the evidence supporting it. Oh, and don't forget the good ol'- fashioned sniff test.
- Information can either be confirmed, denied, or unverified. Don't be afraid to put something in the "unverified" column and reassess its veracity later, after new information is collected.
- Cut out the noise by extracting only the most relevant information.
- Extrapolating information means determining which bits of information can be generalized and

assumed true across multiple scenarios; correlating information is the process of identifying and drawing the connections between seemingly independent data points.

- Having a team that can think creatively and communicate effectively is critical to the extrapolation and correlation phase.
- Collection and analysis never end! The intelligence cycle must keep spinning through completion, even once a decision is made and an action is undertaken.

DECIDE

Choices are the hinges of destiny.
—PYTHAGORAS,
GREEK SIXTH-CENTURY BC PHILOSOPHER

Leave it to an ancient Greek philosopher to boil down the importance of decision making to six succinct words. A high-stakes endeavor is a series of choices, ranging from the tactical choices found in its execution, to the strategic choices made in its management, and all the way to the initial decision to take action—a decision only you, as the leader, can make.

Decisions like this are never easy. It is, perhaps, what keeps so many people from pursuing the road less traveled. The ability to make the decision to act, to take on enormous stakes and pursue great rewards, serves as a gatekeeper—the meek and timid may not pass!

As with anything, there's a right way and a wrong way to approach this range of decisions. It requires you to look upon that intelligence picture you've created and evaluate the risks—more importantly, it requires you to accept those risks. Acceptance is a critical difference lost on many. Success at this juncture also requires that you be willing to act on the imperfect solution. As General George Patton once said, *"A good plan violently executed now is better than a perfect plan next week."*

LESSON 6

Know, Then Accept, Your Risks

Great reward requires great risk. It is an adage that few try to argue with. It is a law that governs capital markets, entrepreneurial endeavors, mergers and acquisitions, and nearly any facet of life—be it business or personal. It is what defines high stakes—and it's what makes high-stakes leadership worth your while.

While few argue with its universal truth, this law speaks differently to different people. To some, it serves as a warning—a cautionary sign that foretells a long and dangerous journey, while barely hinting at the treasures at the end of the road. I think of these people as life managers. A life manager is someone who tries to live his or her existence within a system—a system designed to reduce risk and predict events with relative certainty. They manage this system diligently, avoiding anything that might fluctuate it and cause it to become off balance. They seek guaranteed pensions versus 401(k)s. Pursue defined career tracts versus the career road less traveled. These are the types who travel on organized tours with carefully planned itineraries rather than fly to an unknown country and rent a car or buy a rail pass. I met many people like this in my brief stint in business school. Most of my classmates had the same path charted in their heads. They had just left Financial Firm X (or Consulting Firm Y), where they were an analyst, to get their MBA. They knew that when they graduated, they would be able to join Firm Z as an associate. If they put their nose to the grindstone and worked eighty hours a week, they knew they would make vice president within three years. Once again, if they didn't rock the boat, and simply did their job well enough, they could be confident that another five to six years would bring them a promotion to managing director. Finally, if they managed their teams and systems with precision, they could become one of the select few that rise to the rank of partner. With that, they could be relatively certain that they would make many hundreds of thousands of dollars each year, possibly millions, and live a life of luxury. It's not that life managers are any less likely to be happy and successful, it's just that they tend to achieve that happiness and success in a safe, predictable manner.

Of course, life managers don't just work at the big banks or management consulting firms—they can be cops, or teachers, lawyers, doctors, or assembly line workers—anyone for whom the predictable career path is invariably preferable to the uncertain or unknown. The common thread through all is a dedication to avoiding risk. In many ways life managers are the bedrock of society, because they create stability; they keep the systems working and the trains running on time.

There is a second type of person, however, who views the law of risk and reward through a different lens. To this person, the law is a welcome challenge, not a warning. It beckons them to dare great things. This is the type of person who flies experimental aircraft, or volunteers to ride a rocket into space. This is the person who drops out of Harvard to start Microsoft, or takes out a second mortgage on her home to purchase inventory to fulfill orders for her homespun jewelry business. These people embrace change and assume that risk is only the price of progress. I call these people life leaders because they take great leaps and pull life managers along with them. My calling these individuals life "leaders" should not be misconstrued. It isn't meant to imply that these people necessarily lead teams or giant organizations, although that may be the case; and by the same token it should be noted that life managers are just as apt to lead and inspire others. It simply refers to the fact that, instead of following the path more traveled, life leaders lead themselves, and often others, into risky endeavors and high-stakes situations. They Take Command of their own destiny instead of waiting for an antiquated or established system to dictate their advancement.

I will assume that if you are reading this book you are a life leader—or want to become one. Leading your life instead of managing it is a choice, and with that choice come both rewards and consequences. First the bad: You will often find yourself awake late at night staring at the ceiling—worrying about responsibilities, second-guessing critical decisions made only hours before, listing the endless fires you have to put out the following morning. Many of your days will be spent under a cloud of uncertainty; fear of failure may follow your every move. At times you'll be tempted to envy the certainty and comfort of the life managers around you.

But with all that fear and uncertainty, you will also feel optimism and hope. Excitement at the chance to make an impact. Comfort in your knowledge that underneath all that risk, all that uncertainty, there is a pot of gold (whatever "gold" means to you). The opportunity to live your life the way you see fit. The ability to pursue your dreams unbound by the expectations of others. The freedom to live your life not asking "Why?" but rather "Why not?" As a life leader you'll accept the brief moments in which you envy those following the well-trod path, because in your heart you know that those very same people spend their lifetimes envying your journey.

So you've made the decision. Yours will be a life of challenge and risk taking. You will pursue the less worn path and play life as a high-stakes game. You'll do so because it's who you are; it's in your fabric.

But while it's true that life leaders embrace risk, they don't do so in a blind or reckless fashion. Quite the opposite: They know exactly what they are getting into. They identify the risks. After that? They accept them. They weigh them against the opportunities, and based on that calculus they swiftly determine whether to take bold, decisive action, or whether to hold back. In this chapter, you'll learn how.

Know the Risks

Once you decide to stray from the path of least resistance—whether you want to become an entrepreneur, lead your business unit in a new direction, or advocate for a decision you know will be met with opposition by someone in your organization, the first thing you need to do is assess the risks involved. Analyzing and accepting risk is a constant process that begins in the observation and intelligence phases; however, truly understanding the risk profile you face requires a more complete intelligence picture. Thus, this phase follows the other two because it is that final gut-check prior to making the decision to act. I first became adept at analyzing and assessing risk while in the Marine Corps, and later I translated that skill into my work at Team Rubicon. Disasters, by nature, are a very risky business; and at TR we consistently have to make complicated decisions based on our calculus about various risks that might or might not present themselves. We also know that the only way to help people in desperate need is to assume some of those risks *will* present themselves—and be ready to act, regardless.

In the fall of 2010, monsoon rains caused the Indus River Valley in Pakistan to flood. Within a month, nearly one fifth of Pakistan was underwater, and an estimated twenty million Pakistanis were displaced or affected. United Nations Secretary-General Ban Ki-moon stated that it was the worst disaster he'd ever seen, and immediately requested nearly $500 million in emergency aid. Relief agencies from around the world flocked to the region and spent weeks running clinics and emergency shelters for victims. Team Rubicon, only seven months old at the time, opted not to deploy in the early stages of the disaster. At the time, most of our volunteers were trauma medics, and we were finding it difficult to determine how we might be able to provide aid in a situation that didn't produce any acute injuries, especially given that we didn't have the resources to run a mass sheltering operation.

Our decision changed about a month later, however, when the Pakistani Taliban issued a public statement threatening all foreign aid workers. For unimaginable reasons, the Taliban had vowed that they would begin targeting any foreigners who were delivering aid inside Pakistan. Immediately many nongovernmental organizations and charities began to talk of pulling their workers out of the country, and fears rose that an aid vacuum would be left. That was when I huddled up with William. Despite the fact that we still didn't know exactly what type of aid we could provide, not to mention the fact that the mission had just gotten a whole lot more dangerous, we determined that we would deploy a team to Pakistan, threats or no threats. It sounds crazy, but we had put a lot of time and careful thought into that decision, and a major portion of that was dedicated to a detailed risk assessment.

Clearly, the risks were tremendous. We would be sending non–Urdu speaking Americans into an unstable country that largely despises our existence and had, in no uncertain terms, made it clear our aid was unwelcome. This meant that we would have to limit our visibility on the ground, which made it that much more difficult to spread the word about our services to victims. Furthermore, because most of the area was underwater, we knew that transportation would be challenging—meaning that if we needed to flee a region fast, we might not be able to. Finally, we spent a lot of time discussing what the most catastrophic outcomes could be, and the conversations typically led to the same nightmare scenario—a kidnapping and public execution of one or more of our team, broadcast on the Internet. The risks were indeed grim.

Of course, when assessing risk, you have to rely on more than intuition and imagination—you also need to generate a clear intelligence picture using the cycle discussed in the previous chapter. So we deployed an advance team, which left a few days earlier, to get the lay of the land, establish communication with the local aid groups we would be working with, and gather information to help us assess the levels of risk. Unfortunately, their reports confirmed our worst fears. Almost immediately upon landing and traveling to Lahore, a triple-suicide bombing took place in a market only blocks from their hotel. It was a close call that demonstrated our risk assessment was entirely too real.

Despite our full awareness of these risks, we assembled an incredible team, and tasked them with establishing oral rehydration clinics to mitigate the deaths being caused by water-borne illness and dehydration. We knew that, while the catastrophic outcomes associated with the risks were tremendous, we were uniquely situated as an organization to provide aid because of our prior experience in environments with the same hazards. Our training, we decided, would allow us to operate in a manner that reduced our exposure to these risks; and, quite simply, the potential to save lives was too hard to ignore.

We all hope that the high-stakes situations you face at work and in your personal life don't expose you to the threat of suicide bombs. The point is, as a life leader, you *will* face your own set of unique risks, and in order to succeed you will need to have a thorough understanding of them. Perhaps those risks include an entrenched competitor dragging you into a pricing war, or a struggle with a business partner or collaborator, or an inability to get another round of financing at a critical moment when cash is tight. If you're the kind of person who forges your own path, risks may also extend into your personal life. No matter how successful your career or your business, if it requires you to work one hundred hours a week, will your wife or husband still be around to enjoy it with you? How many baseball games can you miss before your son resents you? These stakes may not be as high as getting severely wounded in an explosion in Lahore, but they are still extremely significant.

For some, analyzing and assessing risk, particularly in business, is a science that involves poring through mountains of data and conducting months, if not years, of research. But, in the world of high-stakes leadership, when time is critical and decisions need to be made fast, we aren't afforded that luxury. So how can we analyze risk both rapidly *and* effectively?

First, we need to understand that there are two dimensions to risk. For some it is convenient to think of risk as binary—it exists or it doesn't. For these people there are no shades of gray. Highly risk-averse people make this mistake all the time, and it's no surprise. It's the "sky is falling" complex. If all you can imagine is the very worst possible outcome, it makes sense that you'd opt to play it safe and do nothing. But in reality, risk lies along a spectrum—two, in fact. Understanding that all risk lies somewhere on spectrums of both severity and probability helps us to more accurately assess and frame what we are facing.

The severity spectrum defines how bad the outcome of any event might be. This generally ranges from negligible (the result will have a barely perceptible impact on you or the organization) to catastrophic (the organization will collapse or lives will be lost). Severity is also relative; for example, a one-million-dollar loss for a business unit at GE might be considered negligible, whereas it would be catastrophic to a young entrepreneur struggling to pay bills. Severity is an extremely dangerous thing to get wrong— for instance, assuming that a third competitor into your market will only result in a 10 percent loss of market share (unacceptable, but not world-ending), when it is in fact 25 percent (catastrophic), can lead to foolhardy risk-taking.

In the Marines, every patrol leader had to identify something referred to as EMDCOA (pronounced *em-dee-co-ah*) prior to going out on a mission. EMDCOA is an acronym that stands for "Enemy's Most Dangerous Course of Action." The EMDCOA forces squad leaders to identify the most severe risks they face—a typical example would be a complex ambush sprung by a large roadside bomb and followed with well-coordinated rocket and machine-gun fire. The outcome of this type of ambush very well could be catastrophic; meaning an entire squad of thirteen men could die or be severely injured. Well-executed ambushes like this were rare—luckily. If they hadn't been, it would have been pretty difficult to convince twenty-year-old men to go out on patrol. EMDCOA, as you can see, deals with severity of risk.

But the probability of the risk matters just as much as the severity—after all, even if a risk has the gravest of consequences, if these consequences only have .001 percent chance of happening, it's probably worth taking the chance. In addition to EMDCOA, the Marines also used a second acronym (nobody ever accused the military of not loving acronyms), EMPCOA (*em-pee-co-ah*), or "Enemy's Most Probable Course of Action."

EMPCOA was equally important, and brings us to the second axis on our risk assessment matrix—probability. The probability scale in military risk assessments ranges from frequent (it will likely happen) to rare (statistically improbable). While leading patrols in Iraq, I discovered that the EMPCOA was, typically, sporadic harassing fire with AK-47s that was (fortunately) fairly inaccurate. Dangerous? Yes, sporadic, inaccurate gunfire could potentially kill a Marine, and no death is trivial; however, in the context of warfare, sporadic gunfire is not considered a catastrophic threat. But because sporadic gunfire was highly probable, it forced squad leaders to expect and plan for it, as well as to know and rehearse standard operating procedures to react to it. Knowing the EMPCOA ensured that they were adequately prepared to respond.

These two spectrums of risk apply equally to all high-stakes situations, especially in business, and it is critical for leaders to not only understand them, but also be able to apply them both proactively (before a critical situation occurs) and reactively (in response to any critical situation that presents itself). Imagine a young Web start-up. First, its founders might recognize that their EMPCOA—the risk most likely to happen—is sporadic server malfunctions due to spikes in Web traffic. In this case the severity of risk is not significant enough to warrant shutting down the company—they are simply careful to add extra engineering staff during peak traffic hours. However, imagine that they determine their EMDCOA—or the worst possible scenario—is a malicious hacker attack that compromises millions of customers' credit card information. Worse yet, the founders realize that they can't build an adequate defense against the attack, making the risk higher on the spectrum of probability. In this instance, it would be prudent for the company to cease operating in that capacity.

It is the ability to reactively assess the risk of emerging situations when the pressure is on, and often with zero advance warning, that really makes leaders and organizations rise above the fray. How often have you seen a leader or organization freeze with indecision at a critical moment? In today's fast-moving business climate, when every second or minute or hour can count, this hesitation can be devastating; and it is very often brought on by an inability to understand the probability and severity of risks faced.

Fortunately, the ability to assess risk is a skill that can be honed through experience and practice. Imagine for a moment that you're a Wall Street trader. The market suddenly begins crashing, and billions of dollars of market cap is pouring off the board as a selling frenzy ensues. You are faced with a choice—you can choose to sell off your positions and hope that the immediate losses you subsume pale in comparison to where the market will end when the dust settles; or you can choose to ride it out and hope that the market will rebound rapidly without your fund realizing any losses. Note that both decisions—waiting and acting— have risks. Only a seasoned trader, one practiced in rapidly analyzing the severity and probability of the risks faced, can make an effective decision in an instant, and he can do this only because his years of experience have taught him exactly *what questions to ask.* What caused the sell-off— market conditions, or extraneous events such as a terrorist attack? Is this an emotional response or rooted in market fundamentals? Have we hedged our market position with other instruments? How likely is it that the information fueling the situation is accurate? In high-stakes situations, knowing what questions to ask often means the difference between paralysis by indecision and taking command.

Another dimension critical to rapid risk analysis is gauging the impact of time; essentially, how is the severity and probability of this risk going to change over a set time horizon? In business, just as in disaster relief and the military, high-stakes situations are not static; they are dynamic, constantly changing and shifting. In order to account for this, leaders must make the following analyses:

1. **How quickly might the hazard emerge?** When we deployed our team to Pakistan in 2010, one prob-

lem was that our most severe hazards—some sort of terrorist attack or suicide bomb—were instant. But there were other less immediate risks to consider: the long-term diplomatic implications if a TR team member was injured or killed by another method during our mission, accountability to our donors if our mission failed for unforeseen reasons, etc. Similarly, in high-stakes business situations, immediate risks can include the loss of a key client, or a plunge in your company's stock price, or an irreversible hit to your or the company's reputation. But other equally severe, equally likely hazards can emerge more gradually—a disgruntled employee suing the company for millions, or a competitor plotting to steal your business, for example. In other words, two risks can have equal severity and probability *right now,* but have entirely different timelines. In general, the more quickly something can emerge, the more catastrophic it can become, since mitigation is more challenging.

2. **How quickly might the hazard change?** For Team Rubicon, the answer to this question is very different if we're tracking a tornado versus a hurricane. Hurricanes have very predictable paths and slowly alter course—the risk conditions shift over the course of days. Tornadoes, on the other hand, can rapidly develop anywhere along a four-hundred-mile storm front, and move erratically and quickly—their risk profile can change within minutes. A great example of a profession that regu-

larly faces rapid shifts in risk is that of surgeons. Most surgical operations go off without a hitch; however, there are few scenarios that have the potential to go from normal to catastrophic in a matter of minutes. Or think of professions that require conducting a lot of negotiations. Most of the time, the negotiation will go smoothly, but on the relatively rare occasion that the person on the other side of the table makes a sudden, unexpected move, you have to be ready to react quickly to minimize the potential for losing the deal or making a bad one. Conversely, risks with a long time horizon include shifts in regulations, public policy, or anything to do with big bureaucracy; for example, if you're a health-care provider, you may know that new regulations are coming, but the precise nature of those changes will evolve and change over the course of months or even years. In general, it's much safer to take on those risks that move slowly, because you'll have more time to test and adjust strategies to cope.

3. **How quickly can we adapt to the change?** That said, if the worst-case scenario—where adapting to the EMDCOA is going to be a Herculean endeavor—requires, let's say, a complete corporate restructuring, or years of lobbying to Congress, or will cost your company billions, it may not be worth it. Looking back at the hurricane-versus-tornado example, if a hurricane's path shifts and it begins moving westward into the Gulf, away from Flor-

ida and toward Mississippi, we would be able to shift personnel and resources within twenty-four hours. However, if a second tornado forms and is bearing down on our team—as was the case in Moore, Oklahoma—we may only have five minutes to move, but we'll likely need fifteen. When the time to adapt exceeds the time it takes for a hazard to change, you're in a bad spot.

In general, the bigger the risk, the more it changes with time, and this requires a constant audit. So you need to constantly be asking yourself:

- Have the potential catastrophic outcomes worsened?
- Is more at risk now than before?
- Has the probability changed?
- Has the reward potential decreased?

These are simple questions that should not impede progress and swift action. Only if the risk has gotten significantly more probable *and* catastrophic should you hesitate, and always be wary of how long that hesitation lasts. High-stakes action both on the battlefield and in business is like a flywheel, and any unnecessary loss in momentum can lower the chances of success.

Accepting Risk

What surprises many leaders is that knowing and understanding risk are only half the battle. Perhaps even more important is *accepting* the risk. What's the difference? The difference between knowing and accepting lies at that critical moment when the chips are on the table and you, as the leader, must make a difficult decision. One option involves hesitation, second-guessing, and perhaps deciding to deviate from a course that only moments prior had been accepted as correct; the risk is simply too great. The second option takes you to that edge of failure, where as a leader you can look over the cliff and see what the consequences would be should the catastrophic happen, but wherein you make the difficult decision and stay the course and take your chances.

What is common between the two options is the presence of fear. What is different is that in the second one you have trumped fear by *accepting* the risk, not just acknowledging it. But how?

Act as Though You've Already Lost What Is on the Line

In 2011 I had the distinct honor of delivering the commencement address to my alma mater, the University of Wisconsin. During the speech I touched on a few subjects, but honed in on one idea—that to succeed in life, it's imperative that we overcome fear and *accept* risk. To get my point across I relayed a story about my time in the Marines. While serving on a scout-sniper team in Afghanistan I was the point man, which, in layman's terms, means that when my small six-man team went out on missions I walked out front—serving as the navigator and chief ambush-sniffer.

It also meant that in one of the most heavily land-mined countries in the world, if there was a roadside bomb or mine in our path I was most likely to discover it in the least desirable of ways—by stepping on it.

Naturally, as a member of an elite unit in a combat zone, I knew the reality I faced. It was a gruesome war. Every single time my unit went outside the wire, there was strong chance of getting grievously wounded or killed. In fact, over the course of our seven-month deployment our unit took twenty dead and over one hundred wounded, with nearly two dozen amputations. None of these statistics were lost on me as I went out night after night to hunt Taliban insurgents—I *knew* the severity *and* the probability of the risks I was facing.

What I soon realized, however, is that there's a stark difference between knowing and accepting. You see, over the first month I began to realize that I was doing a poor job walking point. Though I had no problem getting ready, loading my rifle, studying the maps, and checking the radios prior to patrol, while I was out in front of our six-person team I found myself hesitating. I was patrolling timidly and making sloppy decisions to avoid areas where we needed to go; as a result we were missing checkpoints and time-hacks along the way. I found myself watching the ground in front of my feet instead of the fields in front of my team—and when leading a team through an enemy combat zone, this can be a very costly mistake.

Then, during one particular patrol, on one particularly dangerous route, I failed to notice the hushed calls from my team leader behind me to halt the team. That's when it dawned on me. In essence, I hadn't accepted the risks of my job. While an innocuous incident, it woke me up to the reality that I was so focused on my own safety, I was becoming a liability. At that moment I realized I had to approach my job differently. I had to find a way to go from simply knowing the risks to fully *accepting* the risks. How? *I had to operate as if I'd already lost what was on the line.*

In this case, that meant that I would have to operate as if the most catastrophic outcome—essentially, my getting killed—was a 100 percent probability. It sounds morbid, and extreme, but this was what I needed to do to be able to trust in my training, control what I could, and leave those things I couldn't control to fate. It was only once I changed my mindset about the risks I faced in this way that I began to patrol with confidence and make the tough, right decisions and lead my team to the best of my abilities. Note that I didn't become careless—that's a dangerous mindset. Instead, I became confident.

Leaders in all sorts of organizations, industries, and situations must come to the same terms with the risks they face. Imagine for a moment the classic first-time entrepreneur. She's completed her business plan and analyzed her risks and threats. She has forecasted revenue and expense models, raised a round of financing from friends and family, hired a staff, and opened a personal line of credit. As her business grows, the revenue begins to come in; but with it the risks become more real. Suddenly, she faces a decision—does she self-finance a large production run of her product, or does she timidly continue to conduct market research while the opportunity to become first to market dissipates? Suppose the market conditions haven't changed since the last analysis she conducted; the only shift has been her proximity to the risk. Now it's more real. She feels the growing weight of her employees and investors; and although they all believe in her, she no longer believes in herself. She is well aware that the outcome of her decision could bring her toe-to-toe with failure; meaning her employees might lose their jobs, her investors might lose their money, and she might lose her credibility.

So she has a choice. She can act boldly and do what is necessary for the business, which is to move forward according to plan; or she can act feebly, in order to circumvent the possibility of those risks becoming real. Option one does not guarantee success, but, if made with confidence, it increases the chances. Option two all but guarantees a slow, painful decline in the probability of her business succeeding. But even if she has known the risks all along, if she has not accepted them—meaning come to terms with the reality of what failure looks like—when it comes time to actually act, she freezes.

This is understandable. Whether on the battlefield or in business, it is incredibly difficult to actually pull the trigger on a risky decision until we have fully accepted the EMDCOA—the worst-case consequences. Yet this hesitation is a huge liability for a leader. For one, inaction is almost always worse than action. Furthermore, any indecision a leader demonstrates when standing at a critical juncture can demoralize a team. Teams may be willing to follow their leader off the metaphorical cliff, but they still want to know that a leader has already thought through, identified, *and accepted* the risks of an endeavor prior to taking them to the edge of success or failure. To discover that they have been so loyally following someone seemingly incapable of making difficult decisions will rapidly splinter a group's morale and commitment. Conversely, a leader who has demonstrated a clear understanding and acceptance of risks, who makes decisions quickly, with confidence and conviction, can move teams to commit themselves with fervor—and a fervent attitude is often all that's needed to move the needle from failure to success.

I have been this very entrepreneur. In 2012 I cofounded a technology start-up called POS REP (military jargon for "position report"), and together with my other founders, William and Anthony, raised a seed round of capital in excess of $100,000. Now, mind you, this is not a large sum in the technology space, but we raised it from friends and family, and—unlike with Team Rubicon, where donors know they are giving their money charitably—they wanted it back with a major return on their investment! Sure, we had identified the risks inherent in our venture, yet we were confident that POS REP would be successful, and had every intention of making our investors, and ourselves, some money. As we moved through the early development phase of our beta product, we started to see that many of the risks we'd identified early on were rearing their ugly heads. Our developers were behind schedule, the product had more bugs than we could accept, adoption rates were slower than we'd forecasted. Suddenly, as money in the bank was running low, we had to make some tough choices.

One involved a government contract POS REP had been pursuing with the Department of Veterans Affairs. We had determined that pursuing the contract was in the best long-term interest of the company, but also knew that the work would be time-consuming and challenging. As we began the process it turned out that, sure enough, working with the government was painstaking. We were bleeding cash on legal bills for the contracting process, and we knew we'd run out soon. I suddenly found myself losing a lot of sleep over the fear that I'd have to tell my friends and family that their money was gone. We toyed with the idea of abandoning our course with the VA and moving to some sort of meager ad-based revenue model. But all this would have done was delay the inevitable. Then I realized, after another sleepless night, that I had made the same mistake I had made in Afghanistan. I hadn't accepted what failure looked like. The next day, I recalibrated my mindset and began framing my strategic thinking as if the money was already gone—as if I'd lost all my money, all my friends had stopped speaking to me, and as if every Thanksgiving from that point forward would be incredibly awkward!

It took the Department of Veterans Affairs a year and a half to evaluate and respond to our proposal (don't anticipate finding innovation at the VA!). The response we got was "no thanks." In retrospect, it would seem that we made the wrong choice by opting to try and work with the VA; however, at the time, with the information we had and the situation we faced, it was the right move. But having the guts to pursue it required us to accept the risk that it wouldn't work out.

In today's volatile business world, nothing is more dangerous than ignoring the risk that will almost certainly be inherent in any decision. Taking smart, fast, and decisive action requires that you have identified and evaluated the risk, taken steps to mitigate it, weighed its negative outcomes against positive gains, determined that it is worth accepting, and accepted it as though it were a foregone conclusion. It is a deliberate process that allows you to act and lead with confidence, and perhaps more important, inspire the confidence of those around you.

Back in 2011, while addressing that graduating class of Badgers at the University of Wisconsin, I talked about how the acceptance of risk is what gives us the courage to try and fail. I stated:

> It wasn't until I learned to let go of my fear, to walk those nights with confidence and cool, that I became an effective point man. There were still intersections I had to cross that required me to close my eyes and clench my teeth, but I never stopped pressing on. As you leave here today, you embark on a similar journey—you'll have fewer land mines, but you'll perhaps have more uncertainty. You enter adult life with a downtrodden economy, an uncertain labor market, foreign markets in shambles, and two political parties unwilling to create solutions. You will begin jobs, relationships, and endeavors and come to intersections in life that will make you cringe. You will be tempted to tread cautiously, to hunker down and wait; but I

challenge you to move forward boldly, to live life fully, and to never look back.

This is as true now as it was then, and should be the guiding principle for any life leader who strives to Take Command.

MISSION BRIEF

- Assessing risk requires you to evaluate it along two spectrums: severity and probability. To do so, be sure to think about the EMDCOA—the most severe outcome that could happen; and the EMPCOA—the outcome most likely to happen.
- Risks are sensitive to time. Think about how the risks you face interact with time: How quickly do they emerge; how quickly do they change or shift; and how quickly can you adapt? There's a stark difference between knowing risks and accepting them.
- Fear will still rule your decision making until you accept risks. One good strategy for doing this is to assume that you've already lost what's at stake.

LESSON 7

Find the 80% Solution

William stepped out from behind his desk, which faced mine across the room, and strode deliberately over, placing both palms down on some paperwork in front of me. "Jake," he said, "we need to move. We're wasting time. All our team leaders on the ground are reporting massive devastation. We need to activate nationwide and send them more people."

I nodded my head and glanced at my computer screen; staring back at me was our bank account. "Money is a problem, William. We don't have the money to deploy hundreds of people from around the country—and if we try, it might bankrupt us." The situation was precarious; for the previous weeks I'd been wringing my hands over a diminishing savings-account balance with our director of finance, but this situation provided a seminal moment—the opportunity to prove to the world that Team Rubicon was the real deal. I knew that launching a major operation would bring in a deluge of funding through social media, but only if we attained critical mass before our coffers went dry. "Let's gather the team together and talk through our options."

The team filed in—our director of programs, Joanne; our director of field operations, Andrew; our director of finance, Dipali; and our communications coordinator, Mike. We were a small core team, but we punched above our weight class.

"Andrew, can you brief us on the latest from the teams in the field?" I asked our director of field operations.

For the next five minutes he painted a clear picture of what was happening on the ground. Our teams in the mid-Atlantic had cleared some roads outside of DC and moved up onto the shorelines of New Jersey. There they had linked up with local officials and were continuing to clear roads, expediently repair homes, and come to the aid of local residents. Our teams in New England were doing similar work in Connecticut. Finally, our teams in New York City were working around the clock, helping the city's Office of Emergency Management on tasks ranging from search and rescue to managing dysfunctional emergency shelters. We even had a team, he said, that had established a base of operations in some area of Queens called Far Rockaway— which, we had learned through our sporadic communication with the responders, appeared to be in desperate need of help.

"All right, guys, here's the deal. We need to get more people on the ground, but we have some major gaps that we need to fill. First, money. I'm going to be honest: We only have about four months of cash left at our normal burn; meaning only about four weeks if we launch a major national response. Naturally, the credibility we can glean from this mission will pay financial dividends eventually, but anything short of home-run execution could bankrupt us first. Second, if we're going to deploy a few hundred—or more realistically, a thousand—volunteers, we need to vastly increase our leadership presence on the ground. JC and Pelak are doing great but they're going to need help. Let's start contacting our best TLs and checking their availability. Next we have logistics. This thing has shut down the whole Eastern seaboard. Housing, fuel, food, and water are hard to come by. We need to find a sheltering solution prior to launch; fuel, food, and water we can figure out with boots on the ground. All we're going for here is the eighty-percent plan; money and shelter are the critical trigger points we need to determine prior to launch, the other twenty percent we'll have to figure out on the fly."

"I disagree," one of the team members chimed in. "This place is chaos. We need the hundred-percent solution before we move—that means food, water, fuel, not to mention—"

William cut him off. "That's not how we work. If we wait for things to be perfect we'll find ourselves having this same conversation right here next week."

William was right. In late October 2012, Hurricane Sandy made landfall in the Northeast, bringing with it devastation on a scale that even the most shrewd meteorologists failed to predict. Immediately, Team Rubicon sprang into action, launching eleven response teams spanning from DC to Connecticut. As the first forty-eight hours unfolded, it became increasingly clear that the damage was far greater than initial reports detailed, and Team Rubicon began making preparations to launch its largest operation ever—deploying a thousand military veterans to New York City to lead response efforts.

The scale of what we were trying to do was unprecedented in our young organization. Prior to Sandy, our largest mission had involved only sixty responders; this had the potential to be ten to fifteen times that. We immediately began identifying critical needs: funding, transportation, shelter, food, clean water, and safety equipment for up to a thousand people. Luckily, not long after the conversation outlined above, a number of corporate sponsors rang the phone and offered to finance a large-scale operation, so one critical variable—our lack of funds—was eliminated. Shelter, food, and water still remained unsolved. But we moved forward anyway. Why? Because if we'd waited until we had 100 percent of our plan in place, this massive mission might never have gotten off the ground.

How did we do it? The nature of the situation forced us to get creative. The shelter problem could not be solved by traditional means. All hotels in a thirty-mile radius were sold out; other options, like town halls or community centers, were flooded; and Red Cross shelters were already overwhelmed and overcrowded. Sleeping outside was an option, but with another nor'easter weather system bearing down, and not enough appropriate cold weather equipment, it was a bad one. So I did the only thing I could think of. I began calling the local professional sports teams to see if we could use their indoor practice facilities. Finally, an opportunity arose. An empty warehouse operated by a rock-climbing gym named Brooklyn Boulders was offered up. It was unheated, lacking showers and toilets, cold, and infested with rats, but it would be good enough.

"We're launching," I told the team. "Now."

There was immediate pushback. Some responders were concerned about the safety and comfort levels in the space; others were concerned about other issues and needs that had not yet been identified.

I retorted: "We've covered our critical variables—cash and shelter—plus this is New York. Food might be scarce, and water might be on boil alert, but we can be certain that our teams will not starve. The critical window of opportunity to help and do the most good is now. If we wait to have all the answers, we won't get those boots on the ground until next week."

We launched the team with an imperfect plan. And it worked, better than we ever could have imagined.

What Is the 80% Solution?

Unless you happen to work for a disaster relief organization like Team Rubicon, you're unlikely to find yourself in this exact position on a typical day in your job. Yet, in today's high-octane business world, we *all* frequently find ourselves in situations where the path forward is unclear, the information is incomplete, critical needs remain unmet, and the pressure and hazards are mounting all around. You've assessed and accepted the risks involved, but, without a crystal ball, the accuracy of your assessment is far from guaranteed. You've gathered as much information and intelligence as you can, but you still don't have the complete picture. You have some of the resources, but not 100 percent. You have a partial solution in mind, but haven't mapped it out fully from beginning to end. What do you do?

You act. Individuals and organizations thrive in chaotic, uncertain situations only to the extent that they are able to develop and execute the minimum viable solution and then rapidly iterate off of it. Team Rubicon calls this the 80% Solution, because we've recognized that 80 percent of the solution will get you 95 percent of the way there, and the key to the remaining 5 percent will invariably change en route. Whether in the disaster zone or in business, if you wait to act until you have 100 percent of your information verified, 100 percent of your resources lined up, and 100 percent of your plan in place, you'll likely be spinning your wheels forever. Because as we discussed previously, whether it's a launch of a product that still has some kinks, a marketing plan that hasn't allowed for all possible contingencies, or a financial forecast that's missing key projections, if you're a leader in today's fast-paced, volatile business environment, there is no such thing as a plan launched with 100 percent information.

So what does an 80% Solution look like? It is a loose framework of predetermined standard operating procedures that allow broad flexibility at every level of the organization. It's a nimble, adaptive plan that accounts for both the most likely, and the most dangerous, hazards, but doesn't account for everything in between. It's a mindset that acknowledges that the plan is imperfect and incomplete; but does so knowing that high-stakes situations are fluid and ever-changing, and perfection hardly ever survives first contact with the enemy anyway.

Analysis Paralysis

Time and again, leaders and organizations find reasons not to launch incomplete plans, imperfect solutions, or risky initiatives in the absence of complete information. Excuses born of fear cause them to hesitate. "What if X?" they ask. "If I only knew Y," they comment. There's an industry buzzword for this—"analysis paralysis"—and it's one of the few business buzzwords that isn't overused. Because no matter what industry we're in or what type of job we do, analysis paralysis, unfortunately, is all around us and can be toxic to an organization that is operating in a fluid environment. After all, when stakes are high, people look to their leadership for confidence and decisiveness, and when they see those leaders paralyzed with indecision, they quickly lose confidence in their own chance of success. The irony is that the bolder the plan, the more innovative the solution, the more powerful the idea, the worse the analysis paralysis becomes. So what can we do about it?

Avoiding analysis paralysis begins with culture. Organizations and companies that operate in fast-changing and dynamic industries must be filled with people able to make thoughtful decisions *quickly*—at all levels. This requires being careful about who is brought on board the team (remember, culture is king when building a high-impact team), as well as creating an atmosphere where decision making is nurtured and encouraged. To avoid analysis paralysis, leadership must constantly demonstrate a commitment that praises forward-leaning decision making; one that rewards action over inaction, regardless of success or failure. If team members constantly see mid-level leadership being blasted for taking decisive action that didn't happen to result in success, they'll be more hesitant to take decisive action themselves.

Decisive cultures also require good risk knowledge. Remember the last chapter, about knowing and accepting risk? These skills are critical to building a team or organization that can act even with imperfect resources or information. As discussed earlier, only when individuals and teams know and accept the risks they face can they make necessary high-stakes decisions. Hesitation due to fear of failure doesn't factor in, because they've already accepted the stakes!

One important thing to note is that avoiding analysis paralysis does not always mean making a knee-jerk decision to "act" (whatever "act" might mean for your particular circumstance and industry); it means being *ready* to act even with only 80 percent of a plan in place—and being nimble and flexible enough to adapt this plan as the terrain or conditions change. In fact, it is sometimes critical that the decision *not* to act be made just as quickly and decisively. For example, imagine you're an entrepreneur with a hot new product. Like most hungry entrepreneurs, you've been hitting the streets yourself, pitching your product and getting it on store shelves throughout the region. Suddenly you're approached by a huge distributor who promises to get your product in stores nationwide by the end of the year. Revenues could skyrocket if the distributor delivers, but the distributor is trying to extract a pound of flesh in the deal that will significantly eat at your profit margins—plus you fear that adding a middleman will remove the sense of intimacy you have with customers, something that's been critical to product iteration. What do you do?

A decisive leader would look at the numbers, consult some key advisors, do a gut-check to determine whether the distributor can match its word, and make a decision based on the intelligence he or she has been able to generate. Would this entrepreneur ever have 100 percent of the information needed to make the decision? Of course not. Without a crystal ball, it's impossible to know how well the distributor will make good on his promise, how the wider distribution will affect relationships with customers, or exactly how this will all impact sales. But that leader would gather all the information he can, and make a deliberate decision to act or not to act—in this case, to partner with the distributor or not partner with the distributor—based on the intelligence he has. In either case a decision would be made and relentless execution would follow.

What would an indecisive leader do? Wallow in the uncertainty and wring his hands over the lack of information. He would likely draw out negotiations with the distributor, consult his advisors multiple times (only to likely hear the same advice over and over), spin his wheels drafting sales projection upon sales projection, lose sleep, and drive his employees (who, as part of a start-up, only want clarity of direction moving forward) crazy! All this would serve to accomplish is the distraction of the leader from the activities and decisions that could push the business forward.

The effects of analysis paralysis often linger after the decision has been made. Given all the uncertainty and hand-wringing that went into the decision, an indecisive leader's follow-through usually involves looking backward and second-guessing, rather than looking forward and iterating. Thus the indecision continues!

The better course of action, once the decision has been made, is to execute the plan confidently, then assess the outcome objectively, then be ready to shift gears decisively, as needed.

At this point you might be wondering, How will I know when I have 80—not 60 or 40 or 20—percent of the information? How will I know when it's time to pull the trigger on the idea, implement the plan, or make the game-time decision? You need to look at the number of variables that remain uncertain and untested, and then develop as many contingencies as you possibly can.

Know the Situation Is Fluid

Part of playing in a high-stakes game of business is understanding that virtually every situation of value is in constant flux. After all, every opportunity worth pursuing, every decision worth making, every idea worth exploring comes with a certain degree of uncertainty; if the path forward were obvious, everyone would do it! Crafting a plan under these conditions is like walking down a path where new forks and obstacles in the road appear out of nowhere with every step. As anyone who's ever had to execute a business plan knows full well, risks, opportunities, and resources can rapidly change from the point of decision to the point of action, for better *or* worse. So it's critical that leaders establish a loose, flexible framework that is not dependent on any single variable.

To see how, let's revisit the story about Hurricane Sandy from the beginning of the chapter. As you'll recall, a major unknown variable was the availability of food, water, and fuel. After all, this discussion about whether or not to expand operations was taking place about forty-eight hours after landfall—arguably when things were at their *most* chaotic on the Eastern seaboard. Emergency workers (Team Rubicon included) were only just beginning to conduct initial damage assessments and complete work orders to get basic utilities back online. At this point it was understandable that fuel, for instance, was not available—roads had not yet been cleared of debris, making delivery impossible, and power hadn't yet been restored to the stations, making pumping impossible. We had no way of knowing when fuel might become available; however, what we did know was that the situation would be quickly evolving over the next forty-eight-hour period, and that by the time our larger deployment was activated, launched, and arrived, there was a good chance the fuel situation could have drastically improved. What we also knew was that if the situation *didn't* improve by the time we were on the ground, it would certainly stunt large-scale operations—yet not cause mission failure. We would be forced to wait, but at least would be poised and ready to pounce the moment fuel availability was restored. On the other hand, if we waited for it to be restored before making the decision about whether or not to launch, we would lose those forty-eight hours!

Of course, many other variables could change for the worse during the course of our mission. Recall that one of the critical factors that triggered our launch was the housing solution at a warehouse in Brooklyn. When we made the decision to launch, we had this solution in place, but at any point during our deployment it could have vanished—the warehouse could have flooded, the temperatures could have dropped so low that it was no longer safe to sleep there, or lawyers could have weighed in and advised that it was too much liability for Brooklyn Boulders to carry, for instance.

There was no way to predict and plan for everything that might possibly go wrong; the best we could hope to do was control what we could, and get comfortable with the fact that we might have to figure out the rest on the fly.

What's the best way to operate in a fluid environment? The next chapter will discuss a number of principles that help individuals and organizations not only survive, but thrive in fluid situations. However, prior to ever stepping out into this type of environment, it's critical that leaders instill the right type of mindset in their teams.

I learned a lot about how to do this from my time playing football at Wisconsin under Coach Barry Alvarez, who had a saying, "Control the controllables." What did he mean? Football games are incredibly dynamic, with massive swings in momentum, the opportunity to suffer devastating loss or victory on every play, and plenty of factors that are beyond a team's control. Coach Alvarez, whose blue-collar, "no excuses" attitude and emphasis on discipline were hallmarks of his leadership, demanded that his teams focus only on those factors which they *could* control—attitude, discipline, and execution—and not pay attention to those things that they were powerless over, like bad calls by the referee, or foul weather. This mindset, "control the controllables," instilled in Badger teams a hardiness and self-reliance that ensured energy was expended on worrying only about those things that could be influenced.

The concept of controlling controllables served me well while in the Marines, and it was something I always emphasized to my teams as we ran missions in "uncontrollable" environments. One instance in particular comes to mind. Our sniper team was running a three-day operation in Afghanistan in an attempt to take down the region's top roadside-bomb maker. The mission required us to insert onto a hill outside the range of US forces in the middle of the night, dig concealed firing positions prior to dawn, and then lie in wait for the target to make an appearance. Two huge factors were completely beyond our control. First, it was August in southern Afghanistan, which meant temperatures during the day were hovering between 115 and 120 degrees, and even hotter on the surface where we were lying in wait. Second, the hill that we were digging into in the middle of the night was made entirely of rocks, not dirt, which meant that it took us seven hours to quietly (without the use of a jackhammer or excavator!) dig what amounted to shallow graves in order to conceal ourselves. Both these conditions greatly dented morale and hurt our chances of mission success; yet they were both entirely beyond our control. But rather than bemoaning these conditions, we focused our efforts on the variables we *did* have some control over—the methods of camouflage used to conceal the shallow firing positions, for instance. Focusing on solutions, rather than the obstacles, forced the team to coalesce and get creative, and energized us to act despite the harsh conditions that surrounded us.

In the working world, instilling this attitude can pay huge dividends. When teams and organizations identify and focus on what they can control, they empower themselves to find solutions to overcome those things which they cannot. For instance, entrepreneurs must pay attention to the economy and market conditions—both things beyond their control—but they should not expend effort worrying about them. Rather, they should focus their team's energy on creating the best product or service, the most effective marketing, and the most efficient distribution: variables they can own and influence that have the potential to buoy revenue even in tough times.

So how exactly do leaders and organizations confidently control for these variables within an ever-changing environment? They first eliminate as many variables as they can.

Eliminate Variables

At this point we've been talking a lot about variables. But what is a variable, exactly? Variables are anything that remains uncertain or fluid in dynamic environments; everything from credit markets to government regulations to competitor behavior. Generally, the higher the stakes, the more variables you'll find, adding to the complexity of your decision making. However, just as we all learned in high-school algebra, the easiest way to solve a problem with multiple variables is to isolate and eliminate them one by one, reducing a once complex formula into a much simpler one.

To illustrate how, let's look at our highly complex response to Typhoon Haiyan, which devastated the Philippines in November 2013. In the immediate aftermath of that terrible storm, Team Rubicon quickly activated and deployed a fifteen-person search and rescue team into Leyte Province to begin search, rescue, medical, and assessment operations. Immediately it became clear there were more variables to this complex operation than initially realized. First of all, because the island nation is an archipelago, transportation between the islands was problematic, not to mention the fact that all communication infrastructure was down, and there was barely any food, water, or fuel to be found in affected areas. Furthermore, just as in Haiti, reports of violence and looting pervaded international media. Each one of these facts presented a variable—one that could either improve or disintegrate further while our team was in transit over the Pacific. Additionally, the variables were interconnected and affected one another—for instance, if we ended up having to carry in food, then the team's transportation would be limited to military transport or, even slower, ocean freight. We knew this was a determination we wouldn't be able to make until we arrived;

the best we could do was come up with a flexible plan that could accommodate the various contingencies.

As mission planning progressed, decisions were made to eliminate some variables—and consequently open up possible solutions for others. For example, because we had no way of knowing how much food and water would be available, we decided that each team member would need to travel with enough food and water for a period of seven days. This was accomplished by reducing food intake to one and a half meals per day and providing advanced water filtration systems, all of which could be packed and carried in individual bags. This decision, while far from ideal because it reduced the pack space available for other equipment, not only eliminated the food and water variables for an entire week, but also opened up a broader range of possibilities for another variable, namely transportation. With each member self-sufficient and the team not requiring large freight, their transportation options expanded to include much faster modes of transport, including commercial air, military helicopters, small trucks, and local fishing boats.

In business, eliminating variables does not have to be as reactive as in the above situation; in many cases it can be proactive. Take, for example, a management decision like vertical integration. Manufacturers who are critically reliant on suppliers in their processes can take steps to eliminate variation in quality and dependability by bringing all the stages of the process—from raw material procurement to final packaging—in-house. Likewise, there are steps businesses can take to eliminate some of the variability and uncertainty caused by market conditions; if the consumer credit crunch is causing sales to slow, for example, you could consider using your cash reserves to offer in-house customer financing. Whatever your business challenge, reducing variables in one area will almost always surface solutions in others.

An important tenet of the 80% Solution is the realization that action opens up options. You may recall from the chapter about observation that a critical component of effective observation is changing perspective. Some critical variables simply cannot be seen, or isolated and eliminated, from your current position. Changing perspective often requires some level of forward action or movement. When we deployed to the Philippines after Typhoon Haiyan, for example, we didn't have a 100 percent plan for how to get our team to Tacloban, where it was most needed. We knew that we could get our team to Manila, the capital, which had been unaffected by the storm, but from our vantage point back in the Los Angeles office, how to get the rest of the way remained uncertain. We were in discussion with officials at the Philippine Embassy in the United States, who assured us that they would get us on Philippine Air Force flights going from Manila to Tacloban, yet at the same time we were getting messages from US military officials at the US Embassy casting doubt on whether that would actually be the case. In this instance, we had perhaps even less than 80 percent of the information, but we knew we had to act anyway; the only way to control for the variable was to simply get boots on the ground; to deploy the team to Manila and attempt to get on a PAF flight. But as with any good

80 percent plan, we had contingencies; we sent the team with enough cash that if they failed to board a PAF C-130 transport plane they could either charter a private dual-engine King Air or a slower, fishing-type vessel from a local boat captain. Both those local options, however, could only be sourced on the ground in Manila; you'll hardly find those options online from Los Angeles! Ultimately the team got on a PAF C-130, as originally planned, but we are still certain that showing up in Manila was the only way to verify that it was an option!

What if you can't isolate, reduce, or eliminate a critical variable to a level you are comfortable accepting? What if there *are* no contingencies to your 80 percent plan? First, you must revert back to your risk assessment matrix and answer the following question: Does an adverse outcome for that variable result in a consequence I am unwilling to accept? If so, that's when you make the deliberate, decisive choice *not* to act. In the business world, go/no-go criteria often revolve around financing. You either have the capital to expand your product line, or you don't; you either secure Series B venture money to extend your cash runway and keep the company operating, or you don't. It doesn't always have to be financial, however. Securing a patent or the right partner could just as easily be the critical variable you need to move forward. Needless to say, identifying and communicating trigger points and go/no-go criteria is an important thing for leaders to do—it focuses teams on what really matters. If *no* contingencies exist, inaction may be the best course of action.

Deliberation Can Be Democratized; Leadership Cannot

All right, your team is at the precipice. You've gathered all available information, done what you can to eliminate variables. Now it's time to make a final decision on the course of action. You look around at your team and realize that the next decision made has the potential to significantly impact their jobs, lives, and futures. Make the wrong choice and they could be out of work or lose their homes; make the right choice and the whole team could be rich within a year or two. What do you do?

You're tempted to put it to a vote. After all, with everyone's fate so tightly knit, don't they deserve at least a vote on the decision?

In 2008, my sniper unit was sent to operate in Afghanistan's most hostile province. We were given broad liberties with our rules of engagement, and had nearly carte blanche authority to shoot suspected Taliban operatives. With these liberties came a nearly overwhelming burden of decision making—the kind of decision that required us to weigh our sense of responsibility to protect the Marines we were supporting, and our respect for human life.

Every decision we faced was different, and each presented "evidence" of insurgent activity to a different degree. As the assistant team leader, I would sometimes disagree with our platoon's chief scout, and would advocate taking out a target as opposed to remaining passive and allowing a potential Taliban fighter to walk. It was never a decision I came to lightly, but when I did, I argued it with the fierceness of a Marine trying to keep his fellow brothers safe. Obviously, these decisions had potentially significant repercussions. Taking shots could very well reveal our concealed position, and would put our team in harm's way should a large insurgent force discover where our small team was hiding. Complicating matters further was the fact that our moral consciousness was intertwined. Even though only one of us would take the shot, we would all bear the moral burden of that decision. These were not easy choices for our chief scout to make. But he always made them quickly, confidently, and decisively, and here's how: He always listened, always asked the right questions, and always challenged assumptions. Sometimes a member of the platoon swayed him, other times we did not. At the end of any deliberation, each one of us felt that we had been heard, and that our opinions mattered. *In the end, however, the decision was made by him and him alone.* And, once made, it was final and carried out.

That's how I learned leadership is as much about listening and engaging as it is about deciding and acting. Great leaders know how to manage the dialogue around decision making in order to achieve maximum effectiveness. They poke and prod, challenge assumptions, and always cede ground to good ideas.

When time permits, deliberation is incredibly useful for making decisions in stressful or risky situations. First and most obvious, different perspectives shed light on problems in ways unseen from a single vantage point. Second, deliberation increases team cohesion, because other team members feel heard. When people feel heard, they feel valuable; and when they feel valuable, they perform better.

However, there comes a moment when a strategic decision must be made, and in the absence of a consensus, it must be made by the leader. When the pressure is on and the stakes are high, it's more crucial than ever that the decision be made quickly, communicated effectively, and executed resolutely. That can't happen without strong, decisive leadership. If you've built the kind of high-impact team that recognizes you are prepared, know the consequences, accept the facts, and have heard their views, they will trust your judgment and willingly execute the plan. Deliberation can be democratized; but decision making can't.

Issue the Commander's Intent

You've made your decision; now it's time to communicate clearly to the entire team what your intent is. In the military, this is called a Commander's Intent. Issuing a Commander's Intent is common practice in the military, and it is something that we do regularly at Team Rubicon for large-scale operations and programmatic initiatives alike.

For example, I issued a Commander's Intent for the second wave of responders that deployed to Typhoon Haiyan following the first search and rescue team. It detailed all the critical information, starting with the five Ws (the who, what, where, when, and why of the operation); the ideal end-state as visualized by me (in this case, that we would be able to conduct sustained operations in a safe, cost-effective, and impactful manner that delivered aid commensurate with need); and under what conditions or circumstances we would pull back and cease operations. That Commander's Intent was read, distributed, and publicly posted for all team members to see three days prior to November 17, the launch date of that second wave.

The history of modern-day Commander's Intent is interesting, dating back to the early part of the nineteenth century, when Napoleon Bonaparte changed the face of modern warfare. Whereas traditional armies at the time fought in linear formations, valued strict discipline and blind obedience, and abhorred independent thinking, Napoleon's army favored flexible, disjointed, yet coordinated operations that valued strategic and tactical decision making at lower levels. It was through these unconventional methods that Napoleon's troops crushed once-feared Prussian armies, whose rigid tactics were unable to adapt. Entire units were literally slaughtered while mid-ranking officers waited to be told what to do next. Eventually, the Prussians adopted a philosophy called *Auftragstaktik*— essentially an early version of Commander's Intent. At its core was the realization that chaos reigns supreme on the modern battlefield, and absolute control from high-level command must cede to self-initiated action at lower leadership levels. Today, good military commanders still use Commander's Intent to win battles; it is what enables officers and the noncommissioned officer corps to make complex decisions—often with limited information and resources—that achieve the desired end-state in dynamic and high-stakes environments.

In the workplace, whether you lead a ten-thousand-person organization, a department of twenty, or a team of three, you can utilize a Commander's Intent to help guide teams to successful outcomes. It's important to note that the Commander's Intent is not the battle plan or business plan. It is a big-picture description of what a successful operation and outcome looks like. It provides general parameters to help guide and shape strategic and tactical planning, without dictating it. It is a "North Star" for team members to look at when situations devolve and initial plans go awry. It helps them understand how their CEO or manager envisions the factory floor, the conference center, or any other business "battlefield" at the end of the operation or task. They should be able to look at the Commander's Intent and feel empowered to take initiative and improvise in the face of obstacles, and reach that desired end-state.

Relying on Commander's Intent requires, you guessed it, trust—both of and by the leader. Leaders must trust that team members will only deviate from established plans when necessary and in the best interests of the operations. They must trust that their team is competent and able to execute tasks without micromanagement. By the same token, team members will only be able to execute under the loose mission parameters of Commander's Intent if they trust that their leaders will not second-guess them or, worse, punish them for deviating from the plan when necessary—even if those deviations result in failure. Luckily, if you have built a high-impact team that has established trust through training, transparency, and trials, you shouldn't have to worry about this!

How does this look in business? Take FedEx, one of

the world's most trusted companies, led by its founder and CEO, Fred Smith. Fred Smith is a former Marine, and he built FedEx from the ground up on the premise that a courier could promise more reliability and on-time delivery if it owned its own planes, and didn't rely on other carriers to haul packages (controlling the variables, vertical integration). As such, Fred's Commander's Intent was that every manager do everything within his or her power to make sure packages arrived intact and on time. So what happens when a hurricane threatens road and airport closures in the Southeast's Gulf region? Mid-level managers are empowered to reroute packages, utilize additional aircraft from other regions, double staff at sorting facilities, and so on. Each of these decisions has large implications of cost, liability, and scheduling; but managers make them confidently with the knowledge that they are necessary in order to achieve their Commander's Intent of delivering packages safely and on time. They know that even if an after-action review finds their decisions to be the wrong ones in hindsight, they'll be commended for their initiative rather than punished for their decision (so long as there was not an existing and proven protocol that should have been implemented instead).

That initial search and rescue team that we launched in response to Typhoon Haiyan reached Tacloban just around three days after the storm had made landfall. Team Rubicon at that time was only the second foreign nongovernment organization on the ground in that area, and the only foreign search and rescue team. Weeks later I was asked by a friend at another humanitarian relief organization just how we were able to get there so fast. He said it had taken them an entire week to figure out their food and water supply chain, transportation solutions on the ground, and an assessment of the needs; how were we able to do it sooner? They were shocked when I told them we didn't figure out any of that any sooner; we simply moved forward anyway, knowing that the team we sent was more capable of finding those solutions in Tacloban than if they'd remained in Manila or Los Angeles. More simply put, I told him we'd used the 80% Solution.

Whatever industry or field you're in, and whatever your business objectives are, there are always going to be obstacles, and generally you'll hear more reasons why you shouldn't attempt something than reasons you should. But if you've prepared; if you've built a good team; if you've assessed and accepted the risks; if you have the best intelligence picture that you can hope to generate, then you can be confident that the 80% Solution is enough to act on—whether on the battlefield, amid the calamity of a disaster, or in any high-stakes business environment.

MISSION BRIEF

- The 80% Solution is a loose framework of standard operating procedures that allows a leader to act before waiting for 100 percent of the information to fall into place. We call it the 80% Solution because 80 percent of the plan will get you 95 percent of the way there, and the key to the remaining 5 percent will invariably change en route.

- Analysis paralysis is the inability to act nimbly yet decisively in the face of imperfect information. In fluid, dynamic business environments this is toxic; avoid it at all costs!

- Whenever possible, take steps to eliminate variables. Any action taken to reduce variability opens up options and allows you to build contingencies into your plan.

- While it's important to solicit feedback and multiple perspectives from your team, when it comes time to make and execute a game-time decision, you and you alone as the leader can decide whether or not to act. Deliberation can be democratized; decision making cannot.

- Don't run your business or organization like the Prussians! Empower leadership and problem-solving at all possible levels throughout your institution, and watch as they adapt to dynamic environments with creative solutions to achieve the desired ends.

ACT

*Greatness is not a function of circumstance.
Greatness, it turns out, is largely a matter of
conscious choice, and discipline.*
—JIM COLLINS

You've crossed the threshold. You've figuratively closed
your eyes and gritted your teeth and stepped off in the
face of risk with an imperfect plan.

Success at this stage is part tactics—how you operate
and set your team up for success to get from A to B to
C on its eventual way to F—and part attitude. Great
organizations, whether they're a hot new start-up, a
rock-solid Fortune 500 company, or a champion football
team, have great tactics—they are built around flexibility
while maintaining resolute and disciplined adherence
to guiding principles, whether those principles are
fiscal responsibility, unwavering customer service, or a
commitment to quality.

The second key to successful action is attitude. Coach Alvarez called it "swagger." It was that little extra confidence our teams had that our simple schemes, if executed with toughness, grit, and determination, would overcome any flavor-of-the-day offensive or defensive schemes we faced from opponents. The Marines most certainly have it. That's what allows them to charge headfirst into machine-gun fire and overwhelm an entrenched enemy with pure violence and force—not sophisticated tactics and maneuvers—in what they call "violence of action." At Team Rubicon we call it "tenacity," and believe in it so staunchly that we made it our first of ten organizational values.

In this book we call it "relentless execution"—a conscious choice to succeed; or, rather, a conscious decision not to fail. It's an attitude that is contagious, and has the real potential to change outcomes—no matter the odds.

LESSON 8

Improvise, Adapt, and Overcome

You've prepared yourself. You've built a high-impact team that knows the situation, developed the intelligence picture, and accepted the risks. You've cobbled together 80 percent of the plan. Now it's time to act. But what if things don't go according to plan?

We all know Murphy's Law: "Anything that can go wrong, will." And we've certainly all witnessed that principle in action in our everyday professional lives. Everything was going fine, but suddenly, with the stakes at their highest, Murphy's Law rears its ugly head. Financing falls through. Target performance measures are missed. A key client flees to a competitor. Assumptions—about the state of the market, the health of your balance sheet, the loyalty of your customer base, etc.—have proved to be wrong. Your team's morale is wavering. Your own confidence in your 80% Solution is quickly dissipating and the path forward is unclear. And all around you, those variables beyond your control seem to be closing in.

How can your team press on toward success? How can you stop worrying and start leading?

On June 6, 1944, Allied troops crossed the English Channel by sea and by air in what was, at the time, the largest and boldest airborne and amphibious military operation in the history of mankind. Average citizens often look back upon that day in awe of what was accomplished; it was a victory that saved Europe, and perhaps the modern world. What they often don't realize is all the things that went wrong along the way.

Paratrooper units—which were dropped in behind enemy lines hours before the invasion of the beaches—missed landing zones; got lost in the dark; had units separated, cut off, or comingled; and found themselves in total disarray. Yet, somehow, low-level leaders were still able to muster the initiative to secure the majority of bridges and causeways that had been their original objective. Meanwhile, only a dozen or so miles toward the beach, US Army units were landing in waves on Omaha Beach. That beach, which was heavily fortified and fiercely defended by one of the Germans' best units, quickly became a killing field as machine guns strafed the Americans trying to pour onto the shore. Junior-grade officers were killed or wounded by the dozens, yet units were able figure out a way to breach the seawall. In both instances, the Commander's Intent—whether to secure the inland bridges or to establish a beachhead—was achieved, despite everything going to hell.

Seemingly nothing went right that day, yet victory was ultimately achieved. What had the Army done right that enabled these men to overcome near-impossible odds? How is it that a plan that took years to create was dashed within hours, yet succeeded all the same? Simply put, the Army did what the military does best—it believed in its small-unit leadership and provided those leaders with a tool kit of operational principles that allowed them to improvise, adapt, and ultimately overcome.

THE TOOL KIT

What exactly is in that tool kit? Faith in the strategic corporal, manageable span of control, interoperability, short operational cycles, situational awareness, and a commitment to change when change is necessary.

When I think of adaptability, I think of nimbleness. When I think of what it means to be nimble, I think of small and fast. Think of a gazelle, darting through the leaves, narrowly escaping the grasp of a larger, more lumbering predator. Perhaps think of Barry Sanders, cutting and gliding up and down the football field while hapless defenders twice his slight frame tumble to the ground. You will find throughout this chapter that staying small and fast—both literally and figuratively—are crucial to the principles in this tool kit.

Let's look at each of these in turn, and talk about how you utilize them to build more adaptability and resilience into your team or organization.

Strategic Corporal

The term "strategic corporal" was coined by former Marine General Charles Krulak in the late 1990s to describe the future of leadership as one in which leadership responsibility would be thrust upon lower and lower ranks. At the time, well before the wars in Iraq or Afghanistan, General Krulak foresaw a modern battlefield on which soldiers or Marines would have to simultaneously conduct full-scale warfare, peacekeeping, and humanitarian assistance—all within the same three-block radius, and perhaps all at the same time. This theory, appropriately titled "Three Block War," posited that the only way to lead in these complex, rapidly evolving scenarios would be to empower soldiers ranked as low as corporal to make decisions as complex as whether to open fire on an increasingly hostile crowd; or whether to cease the distribution of aid because of threats of theft. (For contextual purposes, a corporal is the first— i.e., lowest—noncommissioned officer, or NCO, rank. It generally requires just a high-school degree with three or four years in the military, and usually involves the supervision of only three to five individuals—although often more, under certain circumstances.) The reasoning, he proposed, was that conditions would evolve so quickly that guidance solicited from a remote command-and-control unit could very well be outdated by the time it was received—even if modern communications equipment made that communication possible in near-real time. Krulak's theories proved prescient, as the Three Block War he predicted proved all too real in Fallujah and Baghdad ten years later.

In business, just as in the military, a strategic corporal is more than a good leader; it's a good leader with great responsibility *at a low level*. It is the factory floor worker allowed to halt the assembly line if something looks broken; the junior financial officer empowered to influence profit and loss at a level above their pay grade; the production manager able to shift production priorities because of sudden conflicts in scheduling; the assistant marketer encouraged to chime in to save a client pitch that appears to be tanking. Why are these people so important in high-stakes situations? To many it would seem counterintuitive to entrust a junior leader with enormous responsibility when the chips are on the table. However, time and again you'll find that no one understands the nuances of the problem better, has more intimate understanding of the capabilities of the team and equipment, or has a clearer understanding of the situation than the people closest to the action.

I've mentioned the importance of entrusting leadership throughout all organizational levels many times already in this book; but here it will be discussed in practice. The decisions that my sniper team faced in Afghanistan, described in the previous chapter, are a classic example. My chief scout, a sergeant (one rank above corporal), was given the liberty to make decisions that carried enormous weight and consequence for the more than one thousand Marines in our battalion, yet he was not asked to run those decisions past our battalion commander. Rather, he took the strategic guidance, rules of engagement, and Commander's Intent, and was empowered to make the decision on his own. Likewise, in the absence of my chief scout's direct input or guidance, I would have been empowered by him to make the exact same call. Adopting the concept of the strategic corporal in your own organization requires adherence to many of the principles already discussed—all employees must be prepared and trusted; they must know the full intelligence picture and assess and accept the risks of their own actions; and they must be able and willing to work off the 80% Solution. If you haven't figured it out, the strategic corporal is essentially what empowers everyone in your organization to carry out the Commander's Intent.

On D-day, one of the main reasons the mission succeeded despite the odds was because the low-level leaders acted with a level of authority and decisiveness usually reserved for leaders above their pay scale. Indeed, it was the lowest-level commissioned and noncommissioned officers who were able to muster the initiative to secure the majority of bridges and causeways, and it was the junior-grade officers who were able figure out a way to breach the seawall. In both instances it was thanks to their leadership that the Commander's Intents—first to secure the inland bridges, then later to take control of the beachhead—were achieved despite everything else going to hell.

Strategic corporals are critical to just about any business. In your case, they might be managers empowered to deftly handle customer meltdowns with decisive customer service. They might be the junior analysts given permission to hit the emergency brake on trading when markets go awry. Or they might be everyone on the front lines, serving customers—like the manager and drivers in the FedEx example from the previous chapter—empowered to make critical profit-and-loss-impacting decisions when foul weather threatens the company's ability to fulfill their promise to customers.

In 2013 Team Rubicon responded to terrible flooding in the cities and communities just north of Denver, Colorado. These communities had not seen flooding like this in decades, and were caught entirely off guard. Over the course of about three weeks, Team Rubicon's Region 8 maintained a large-scale flood-recovery operation that focused on providing disaster assessments and intelligence, as well as critical home salvage work, which included gutting flood-damaged homes so that deadly black mold didn't set in before the ice-cold winter. At one point during the operation, one of our newest junior strike-team leaders was approached by a family who said their elderly father's home, which was cut off from vehicle access because of a washed-out bridge, was already showing signs of deadly mold. This strike-team leader, despite lacking significant experience with the organization, an official work order from the Operations Section, or even the ideal equipment, nonetheless made the decision to have her team carry all the tools available on their backs, and travel on foot a few miles into the wilderness along poorly maintained trails and across rushing streams, in order to help the family. She felt confident in doing so because she knew Team Rubicon valued initiative and individual judgment—which we did.

Think about your own organization and team members. Do you have strategic corporals? Do they feel empowered to make critical decisions? How can you tell? Well, if your people only tell you about problems *after* they've solved them, you can rest assured you've set the right tone and recruited the right people. If you hear about every problem as it occurs and are asked to weigh in with a recommendation, I recommend you hit the reset button. Either you have done a poor job facilitating an environment of trust and encouragement, or you've built the wrong team.

Span of Control

But it's not just enough to empower everyone to make critical decisions within their control; it's also critical that the span of their control be both clearly defined and manageable. Span of control simply refers to the number of people that any single individual is responsible for leading. In the military, span of control is both small and strictly delineated. A fire-team leader leads three men; a squad leader leads three fire-team leaders; a platoon commander leads three squads; a company commander leads three to four platoons; and so on, all the way to the commanding general.

Keeping the span of control relatively small ensures that the immediate leader or supervisor has the ability to maintain direct and effective command over his or her subordinates. Having too many direct reports is sure to overwhelm a leader, or force her to direct an inordinate amount of attention to only a subset, leaving the rest unattended. This of course means that, inevitably, issues go unaddressed or opportunities get missed. The opposite situation, in which a leader is assigned *too* small of a team, creates inefficiencies. In that scenario, either the leader's responsibilities could or should be absorbed by his superior, or he should be assigned a larger staff.

In business, too, span of control should never expand beyond more than three to seven direct reports; if you find that leaders in your organization are being held responsible for teams much larger, you should immediately find a way to break those teams into small, more manageable and modular groups. During the second phase of the response to Typhoon Haiyan, for example, Team Rubicon had deployed a Disaster Medical Assistance Team (DMAT), a medical strike team, an engineering team, and a support team. The DMAT consisted of twenty-six medical professionals, but was capable of operating in multiple smaller units. So after assessing the situation in Tacloban, the hardest-hit area, commanders on the ground determined that the DMAT should split, and half the team should travel to a small town called Carigara. Once in Carigara, the DMAT detachment leader determined that the thirteen-member team should further separate into two elements—one to be stationed at the hospital and one at a clinic in the community center. Meanwhile, back in Tacloban, the chief medical officer and the medical strike-team leader decided to further break up the remaining team into small foot-mobile medical patrols, and deploy them to reach immobile populations in the Barangays. Being able to treat the DMAT as a set of modular medical units, rather than one unwieldy whole, enabled commanders on the ground to adapt more quickly to the ever-changing situation and conditions, and make faster decisions that maximized impact over a broader area.

No matter how big or small your organization, span of control is just as critical in business as it is during a typhoon response. This is why some of the most nimble and adaptive companies, such as 3M, have adopted "matrix organizational structures," in which individuals in functional areas, let's say engineering or finance, officially report to a functional manager, but are placed on product- or project-specific, cross-functional teams with a different manager. It might sound inefficient, but in reality decoupling formal leadership (the managers people officially report to) from informal leadership (the managers whose advice and guidance people seek on a day-to-day level) gives leaders the luxury of rapidly reconfiguring teams as needed —creating or dismissing them, expanding or contracting—in an ever-changing industry environment. If they suddenly sense a new market opportunity, for example, they can quickly cobble together a team to exploit it, while a more traditional and clunky organization might take weeks to build a new division simply to *explore* the possibility.

Of course, when you have lots of small, nimble teams working in concert, good communication and coordination across—not just within—operations is key. In essence, when you are constantly and rapidly creating new business units or special project teams with individuals who may or may not have worked together before, it is critical to continuously ask: Is everyone and everything on the same sheet of music?

Few examples highlight the perils of poor communication across operations more starkly than the response to the terrorists attacks on September 11, 2001. Unimagin-

of the flexibility achieved by our small span of control with NIMS, and the plug-and-play interoperability it allows, we know that our teams are fast and nimble and can adjust to the size and complexity of incidents as needed.

If you are or plan to run a matrixed team or organization, have you established common operating guidelines and language? When team members coalesce to take on a new time-critical project, do they spend the first three days determining who will play what role and what the definition of a "widget" is, or do they have the baseline knowledge and vocabulary to hit the ground running? There are huge efficiencies to establishing common standards, whether that means creating templates for reports, establishing a report or meeting rhythm, or working off a common vernacular.

Equipment Interoperability

The interoperability of equipment is just as critical, whether you lead a team responding to a typhoon in the Philippines or at a research and development facility in New Jersey. As simple as this sounds, it's often the most difficult component to get right. Take, for instance, the high-tech communications and assessment equipment we took to Typhoon Haiyan. As discussed before, space and weight were at a premium because of our need to carry in our own food. Despite this, we knew that communication would be critical in the early stages of the response, in order to help provide information that would shape follow-on teams. Once on the ground in Tacloban, our team's communications leader

ably, according to reports released after the attack, police, fire, and city officials responding to the scene at the World Trade Center couldn't even speak to one another over the radio because they had never predetermined common command-and-control radio frequencies. Furthermore, no thought had been given to what a common command-and-control structure would look like if multiple agencies responded to a massive event like the one they found in Manhattan. Fortunately, this hard-learned lesson sparked the creation of the National Incident Management System (NIMS). Among other things, NIMS ensures that when various disaster response "pieces" come together for a complex response, everyone is working off a common command structure, utilizing common language, and has interoperable equipment.

You too can implement your own version of NIMS in your team or organization. Team Rubicon fully adopted NIMS as its operating framework in late 2012 after realizing that though our members had a common background and training in the military, assembling teams from across regions and states to respond to disasters was proving too difficult. Additionally, much like when the various departments arrived on scene after 9/11, when we showed up to disasters across the country we were not always speaking the same language as the government agencies we were interfacing with. Now, when volunteers arrive on scene they know to expect to be tasked out to a strike team, which will be led by a strike-team leader, who will receive guidance from the Operations Section, which is working off intelligence created by the Planning Section, and so on. Because

began setting up the satellite terminal. When it came time to link it to his laptop, we identified a critical error—the cable for the terminal would only link to a PC, and he had a Mac. Cue forehead slap! Later, with the second wave of responders, we realized that our Palantir mobile devices (cell phones loaded with intelligence and assessment software from Palantir Technologies) were not all operating on the same version of the software, making them unable to operate together. Luckily neither of these failures was catastrophic to mission outcomes, but they both created massive inefficiencies that reduced our ability to operate nimbly and independently.

How can equipment interoperability affect you or your organization? Let's revisit two corporate examples used in prior chapters. Recall how FedEx empowers all employees to take any action necessary (within reason) to achieve the Commander's Intent of always on-time package delivery? In that example, one measure a facilities manager might take is to reroute planes in advance in anticipation of poor weather conditions. Well, imagine that FedEx rerouted a plane from Memphis to Atlanta, only to learn that they have to call in a second flight crew (the existing flight crew had to take a mandatory twelve-hour rest period before flying again). So the FedEx manager calls in a second flight crew, but upon arrival it's discovered that the planes FedEx dispatches from Memphis are different than the planes dispatched from Atlanta—and the new pilot is not licensed on the type of plane brought in from Memphis! Contrast this with Southwest Airlines, which only flies one type of plane. There are many reasons that they've been profitable year after year, but the fact that Southwest Airlines only flies one type of aircraft—allowing any pilot, mechanic, or flight attendant to work on any plane, for any route, at any time—can certainly be credited with contributing to their reputation for punctuality and dependability. Of course I'm just using this as a hypothetical example (I have no idea if FedEx has different planes flying out of different locations), but it paints a clear picture of the importance of using the same operating equipment across the organization—or, at a minimum, of ensuring that everyone is cross-trained on the various equipment implemented.

The bottom line? Interoperability creates simplicity. Simplicity reduces confusion. Less confusion means more agility, and the more agile you are, the more likely you are to succeed under volatile conditions.

Shorten Your Operational Cycle

The first skill they test in Marine Sniper School is land navigation by map and compass—both in daylight and at night. Carrying a sixty-pound pack, you are launched into the wilderness in search of eight different grid coordinates spread across the mountainous and wooded terrain of Camp Pendleton, each one marked on the ground by a single, four-foot-tall stake. Looking at the map, you know where you are, and you know where the stake is supposed to be, but getting there is not as simple as drawing a straight line across ten kilometers of rugged terrain. You see, invariably, between you and the stake lies a steep mountain ridge, a large body of water, or an impenetrable thicket of vegetation, not to mention any of the unknown obstacles that are certain to pop up en route.

The natural response is to immediately start trying to map that ten-kilometer route, from beginning to end. But what if, instead, you break the journey up into manageable legs? What if each leg becomes a benchmark at which you'll evaluate your next course of action according to the situation? You don't try to get from A to Z in one journey; instead, you set Z as the goal, and then focus on getting to D by moving from A to B to C. At D you reevaluate, and start the process over again.

Chaotic environments are a lot like land navigation. You might have a map (your intelligence picture), which may or may not be accurate. On that map you see some of the obstacles in your path, but you know that the map's level of detail doesn't reveal everything you'll encounter. You develop a plan, which may or may not need to be changed. So how do you succeed? You shorten your operational cycle. Instead of trying to achieve the ultimate goal all in one shot, you set yourself lots of mini goals that inch you closer and closer to the desired end-state.

The temptation in chaotic or uncertain environments is to try to take too much on at once, but this inevitably leads to teams becoming overwhelmed. By reducing your operational cycles into manageable chunks you can decrease uncertainty, increase situational awareness, and keep your head above water. Additionally, artificially breaking major goals—whether it's a sales target, the completion of a major research project, or a huge product launch—into more easily accomplished benchmarks provides the opportunity for small "wins," which are critical to increasing a team's confidence and improving morale. Successfully completing a leg, in other words, instills confidence and gets you one step closer to that elusive stake. Because of this, it's critical to reduce operational periods—the period of time that is planned for and executed prior to iteration—accordingly. These operational cycles, or operational periods, can either be time based (say, a twelve- or twenty-four-hour period) or goal based (the first ten of one hundred units sold).

Many participants of elite military schools—be it Sniper School, SEAL/BUDs training, or the Special Forces Qualification Course—unconsciously use this tactic to get through grueling periods of training. I certainly did. While in Sniper School, where every day was a marathon of misery, I found myself reducing my operational periods to the time between meals. "Just make it to lunch," I would think to myself in order to get through a midmorning exercise. And when lunch would come, I would immediately shift focus to making it to dinner.

Deliberately manipulating your operational cycle—whether measured in time, like a week or four hours, or in progress, like 10 percent or 25 percent of the goal—allows you to consciously force yourself to reevaluate the situation, your advancement, and your hypotheses about what your next steps should look like. In order to maximize the effectiveness of short operational cycles, you must be continuously looping through your intelligence cycle, adding in all the new information you are observing and data you are collecting. Remember, you may not have started the journey with a perfect plan or intelligence picture, but you should be constantly improving it along the way.

Of course all this intelligence gathering is only worthwhile if you are willing to adjust course. As the situation changes—as information comes to light or assumptions are proved wrong—strong leaders and flexible organizations must be *willing and ready* to adapt. Rigidity based on pride or fear is unacceptable, and will most assuredly end in failure.

Some Marines, however, never navigated in the way described above. Instead, they used a technique called dead (or "ded") reckoning. Dead reckoning requires a navigator to start from a known location, from which he uses his compass to shoot an azimuth (an angular distance from north, expressed in degrees) toward his destination, say 45 degrees (since 0 degrees is North, and 90 degrees is East, this would be a NE direction). Then, the navigator looks at his map and measures the distance he must travel to the goal, let's say it is 2,200 meters away (a little over a mile). Now, knowing direction and distance, the Marine steps off. Since he's not using GPS, he has to use his "pace count" to determine how far he's gone. A pace count is the precise number of steps that an individual Marine takes for every 100 meters traveled; naturally, each Marine has a different pace count. So, here travels the Marine, staring at his compass, ensuring that the compass's index line does not deviate from 45 degrees, while silently counting his steps in his head, marking off every 100 meters on his way to 2,200 meters.

As you can guess, this is the least tactical navigation method imaginable! Most obviously, dead reckoning never forces you to pause and measure progress. As a result, small errors made in the beginning are massively compounded over the course of the trek. An error of a few degrees at the onset of the journey will potentially leave a navigator hundreds of meters off his target by the time he's walked the full 2,200 meters; by then it's too late! Perhaps even worse, because dead reckoning requires the Marine to keep his eyes on his compass, he is not observing what is around him or, more importantly, what is in front of him. Before he knows it he's walking straight into a lake or off a cliff or, worse, into an ambush.

The parallels to business are easy to see. Imagine the entrepreneur setting a pricing strategy for a new product. Selling a thousand units in the first quarter will achieve a 20 percent return on his initial investment, and that is the target he sets his sights to hit. Knowing his goal is one thousand units, he puts his nose to the grindstone alongside his sales team. The product is selling well, but through the first two months of the quarter, he's on pace to sell only nine hundred units. Knowing he has to work extra hard to meet the goal, he starts paying his team overtime.

The quarter ends and he learns that he's sold 1,015 units; victory! Not so fast. His accountant tells him that the company lost money on the quarter. He soon learns that the overtime costs ate into his profit margins, and his assumptions modeled at the beginning of the quarter on the number of items returned or exchanged was grossly underestimated. After a deeper postmortem, he learns that two individuals on his eight-person sales team accounted for 50 percent of all the sales; yet because he'd never paused to reassess strategy he never learned of their successful technique, and thus failed to share it with the other salesmen.

Upon reflection, he realizes that if he had broken his goal into shorter operational periods, he could have significantly increased efficiencies on his sales team, thereby avoiding those overtime costs in the third month. He also could have made adjustments to account for the erroneous returns and exchanges assumptions, allowing him to better forecast through the rest of the quarter.

Whether your goal is hitting a sales target, navigating difficult terrain (literal or figurative), or something non–business related entirely, like finishing a marathon or losing those last twenty pounds, I can't stress enough how critical it is to break down large, long, or complex tasks into manageable units. As a leader, maintaining situational awareness of the present situation while keeping one eye focused on the horizon allows your strategic corporals to tackle immediate challenges head-on, achieving a drumbeat of steady victories while staying nimble enough to change course as unexpected obstacles or opportunities arise.

Control the Dialogue

If you're not talking, the saying goes, somebody else is; and you likely can't control what they're saying. In today's hyper-transparent world, what people are saying about your business—not just outside but also within your organization—can be critical to either your success or failure. As the leader, only you can dictate which it is.

At Team Rubicon we control the dialogue by being deliberate in the communication we use to inspire our volunteers. We celebrate and share the small victories we rack up in addition to the big ones, and as a result, our volunteers and donors don't see our goals as daunting tasks; they see a history of success and thus are inspired with a corresponding confidence and poise that breeds further success. But controlling the dialogue has another benefit. Since we're constantly pushing rich and engaging information about our progress at our volunteer base, they don't ever go looking for it, which means they won't come across the occasional detractor or critic (though of course at headquarters we stay attuned to those, and are transparent when legitimate criticism emerges) that might make a dent in their morale.

In high-pressure situations in particular, one way to control the dialogue is to establish a set chain of communication whereby employees report mission-critical information only to their direct superior. Why? For one, when individuals are speaking out of their chain of command, it can cloud the picture that leadership is trying to paint. This doesn't mean that every employee shouldn't be able to speak her mind—she should—simply that she should follow the proper protocol. Plus, no matter what your business, it's safe to assume that as stakes and uncertainty increase, there will be a corresponding increase in fear in some of your team members. Fear usually leads to speculation, and speculation inevitably leads to rumors. Nothing will ruin a team's unity of effort quicker than a toxic rumor mill. This is why it is also imperative that you not allow employees who are not in the know to *act* like they're in the know. Once alerted to rumors or breaks in the communication chain, you must move to swiftly and decisively squash them.

This came into play for me during our mission to the Philippines. I was located with our logistics element in Manila, helping to solidify some of the political relationships needed in order to sustain operations. A few days after I arrived, our DMAT team arrived, and it was critical that they get down to Tacloban as soon as possible in order to maximize their medical impact on the ground. The problem was that I was receiving conflicting information from our team on the ground about where to send them. Our first search and rescue element, at this point back in the US, had scouted a town called Carigara an hour outside of Tacloban and determined that it would be the best place to send our team. That assessment, however, was not agreed upon by certain members of the team. When a second team arrived and scouted Carigara, there was once again dissention among the members as to the value of sending the DMAT there.

What was important to me in both cases was that despite the dissention within the teams, each *team leader* believed Carigara to be a credible mission, and I had worked with each of these team leaders in the past. I knew how they thought and how they communicated, and if their assessment was that Carigara was the mission, then that's all I needed to hear. Nonetheless, other members of the team began circulating rumors that it would be a waste of time, and on multiple occasions broke the chain of command by calling me or my deputy directly to offer their own "assessments." The moment I received those phone calls I sternly told the team member on the other end of the line to hang up and speak directly to their team leader. Their team leader, I assured them, would hear them out and report up to me what was relevant. Next, after learning that the DMAT was hearing these reports as well, and subsequently second-guessing whether we as leadership were sending them on a wild-goose chase, I gathered them all together and addressed the concerns head-on. I didn't deny that there was disagreement among some about the validity of Carigara, but I assured them that we were operating with a clear intelligence picture that was generated by our most trusted team leaders in the organization. It worked. Oh, and the portion of our team that headed to Carigara saw nearly a thousand patients, performed hundreds of surgeries, and delivered multiple babies.

Truthfully, controlling channels of communication is one of the most critical components of high-stakes situations. Understandably, all your employees are going to want to share their perspectives—and in the right forum that is good, and should be solicited—but when unsolicited and coming at the wrong time, it can be toxic. To combat this you have to establish clear lines of communication and enforce them. Never allow your subordinates to jump the chain of command in the midst of these situations (different from the steady-state transparency and open-door policies discussed earlier). The reason this is so important is because you will by now have a long-standing relationship with your leaders—you'll know how they communicate, what they tend to exaggerate, or what they'll typically omit. As a result, you'll know how to filter what you're hearing from them or ask probing questions to get the facts that you suspect they are glossing over. When you're getting unsolicited information from someone you don't have as much history with, it's difficult to judge what lens they are observing through, and as such it's a challenge to know how much weight to place on what you're hearing. Also, while the rumor mill among employees is inevitable, as the leader it is critical you not be influenced by it—or allow your team members or employees to be, either.

The best way to control communication is to own how you communicate—to communicate clearly, transparently, and frequently hit the messages you want to be heard, so regularly that your people hear you in their sleep. Commit to it. If you don't control the dialogue, someone else will.

The principles found in this chapter, if instituted early and adhered to relentlessly, will help increase your chances of success when you embark on your high-stakes endeavor. Of course, nothing can ever guarantee success, nor will any amount of preparation ever make it easy. However, it's the challenge and the risk that draws us to these endeavors to begin with. If that weren't the case, it would be a much more crowded field and we'd hardly be blazing a trail.

Now we are going to conclude with just one more lesson, and it's not something you can write into a business plan or adopt as a standard operating procedure. It's called "relentless execution," and it is ultimately what separates the winners from the losers.

MISSION BRIEF

- In high-stakes situations in particular, if something can go wrong, it will. Build your team or organization around a tool kit that maximizes its flexibility in the face of uncertainty.
- Relying on strategic corporals makes you a better leader and ensures decisions are being made closest to the issue at hand—where they belong.
- Keep everyone's span of control manageable and small; when leaders have too many responsibilities and direct reports under their purview, it creates inefficiencies and breakdowns.
- Strive to keep your information, your operating procedures and equipment, and your vocabulary consistent across all teams, departments, and units; this will maximize your ability to reconfigure teams at a moment's notice and remain flexible under changing conditions.
- Make the large small; the complex simple. Shorten your operational cycle and go for quick, easy wins to improve morale.
- Own the dialogue. Period.

plan in a way that convinced people—people he didn't even know—to follow him? And what was the key to the group's success only minutes after he shouted his famous words, "Let's roll"?

We don't know all the details of exactly what went down on that infamous day, but we do know that against impossible odds, and with the highest stakes possible, Todd Beamer rose to the challenge. He hastily constructed a plan to overpower the terrorists, communicated the course of action clearly and decisively to the passengers, then led that group of passengers to implement it with ruthless determination. Did Beamer have every element of the plan in place at the moment he decided to take action? Of course not; as you've read about throughout this book, when the stakes are at their highest, there is no such thing as a foolproof plan.

So how did he succeed? How, when it was all on the line, and none of the desired pieces were in place, did he overcome seemingly impossible odds?

Expert analysis has pieced together the final moments before United 93 went down and determined that, just prior to the plane crashing into a Pennsylvania field, Todd and the team of uprising passengers hit an insurmountable obstacle—the terrorists had locked themselves in the cockpit behind a locked metal door that seemingly couldn't be breeched. To make matters worse, the passengers had no idea how many terrorists were hiding behind the locked door, what kinds of weapons they had, or even what their motives were in hijacking the plane. Yet even though the pressure couldn't have been higher, the information in-

CONCLUSION

On September 11, 2001, Todd Beamer boarded United Air lines Flight 93 like every other passenger—dreading the cross-country flight to San Francisco. The last thing he ever expected he would do that day was have to inspire a handful of terrified passengers to forcibly wrest back control of the plane from a group of terrorists hell-bent on crashing it into our nation's capital, and save hundreds, maybe thousands, of lives in the process. Yet that is exactly what he accomplished.

What inspired Todd Beamer—just a regular guy with no official leadership role, no particular knowledge of how to operate a complex aircraft, and no special crisis-management training—to step up at that moment and Take Command? How did he inspire such heroic action from other ordinary people around him? How did he rise above the panic and chaos of the moment and formulate a plan despite having only limited information, limited resources, and limited time? How could he have possibly communicated that

complete, and the outcome uncertain, Todd Beamer still *chose* success over failure. He ordered those around him to turn the attendant's beverage cart into a battering ram, and together they relentlessly pounded that door with all their might until one of two things happened: They either broke the door down and entered the cockpit, eventually overpowering the hijackers, or the hijackers, knowing that the collective will of the passengers would soon overcome them, elected to crash the plane into the field themselves. In either scenario, the passengers succeeded.

The key takeaway here is that Todd Beamer and his team *chose* to succeed. Instead of simply sitting back passively and resigning themselves, as many would have done, to the fact that they would probably not survive the terrorist hijacking, they instead opted to stand up and Take Command of their fates, and the fates of those whose lives they saved on the ground.

Whether in a hostage situation, in the disaster zone, or in the hectic everyday world of work, the magic ingredient that makes the seemingly impossible possible—that allows us to succeed when the probability of failure is highest—is relentless execution. It was the power behind everything from the stunning victory of the 1980 US Olympic hockey team to the victory of the Allied troops in the Battle of Normandy. It is the sauce behind Southwest's unexpected rise against airline-industry titans. It is Steve Jobs getting fired from Apple and going on to revolutionize the entire personal computing industry, or Elon Musk pouring nearly his entire personal wealth into building cleaner electric cars and faster rocket ships—things everyone said simply couldn't be done—and becoming an industry titan in the process. It is the discovery of a vaccine for polio, the end of apartheid in South Africa, the triumph of Apollo 13.

In the business world and beyond, relentless execution is what's needed in that moment when the chips are on the table and you've done everything in your power to put yourself in a place to win, only to see the opponent draw an ace on the river card. It is what's needed at the moment when you stare fate in the face and laugh, because you suddenly realize that the whole notion of "fate" is a myth—that you're the only person who can control where you go from here. It's the difference between success and failure at the moment of truth; that moment when you are called upon to stand up, Take Command, and inspire those around you to do the same.

RELENTLESS EXECUTION

I have only two men out of my company and twenty out of some other company. We need support, but it is almost suicide to try to get it here as we are swept by machine-gun fire and a constant barrage is on us. I have no one on my left and only a few on my right. I will hold.

—FIRST LIEUTENANT CLIFTON B. CATES, USMC, IN A REPORT WRITTEN AT THE BATTLE OF BELLEAU WOOD, JULY 19, 1918

The above quote is a part of Marine Corps lore. Lieutenant Cates, a junior grade officer, was holding a line of Marines in the face of a fierce German onslaught. This battle, the Battle of Belleau Wood, was one of the bloodiest of World War I, and in it the Marines earned their legendary nickname, *Teufel Hunden,* German for "Devil Dogs." The Germans gave them this nickname because from their perspective there was no way the Marines, whom they outnumbered and outgunned, should have defeated them that day; the only explanation that German officers had to offer for their defeat was that they met a foe that "fought like dogs from hell."

Lieutenant Cates, who scribbled the quote above on a filthy piece of paper and had a courier run it back to the command post, wasn't even supposed to be in command that day. He had simply found himself in a critical position of leadership after his company commander was killed. Despite his entire unit being at 15 percent strength and piecemealed with other units, he took command. His final words on that note, "I will hold," perfectly demonstrate the spirit of relentless execution. He had nearly none of his own men, was outnumbered and suffering a withering barrage of artillery and machine-gun fire, yet *damn it,* he was a Marine, and Marines don't lose battles. Cates didn't hold that line by accident or luck; he held that line by refusing to accept failure.

There have been many times when Team Rubicon has had to rely on relentless execution to keep the organization alive in the face of seemingly insurmountable obstacles. For example, in early 2011, barely a year after we were founded, things seemed to be going well. We'd just wrapped up five successful overseas missions in Haiti, Chile, Pakistan, Burma, and South Sudan. With the early success of those missions, we convinced a very successful businessman to contribute $100,000 to our fledgling nonprofit start-up. William and I, still working without pay, felt confident that it was time to launch into growth mode and bring on board our first full-time employee, and hired a woman named Joanne on the expectation of receiving those funds.

Fate had a different plan. The businessman, without explanation or cause, pulled the funding commitment and we suddenly found ourselves staring at a bank account that could only keep us going for less than ten weeks—if no disasters struck in between. We had no safety net. William had hastily packed up his life in Washington, DC, and moved to Los Angeles, and was renting a converted garage as an apartment; and I, two months prior, had walked away from a full-ride scholarship at UCLA's MBA program after one semester, and was living on a shoestring. Yet we were committed. We had already analyzed and accepted the risks of our endeavor. We relentlessly doubled our efforts, taking every meeting that came our way. Tirelessly and without pay, we worked days, nights, and weekends to make sure that when our break did come—and we maintained our faith that it would—we'd be ready.

Two short weeks later, a devastating tornado tore through Tuscaloosa, Alabama. We had never run a domestic operation prior to this moment, but as we watched the destruction on TV, we knew that we could help in some way. Quickly, we built a hasty plan and activated a team. We arrived in Tuscaloosa without domestic protocols and without the right tools, but with an unrelenting desire to help. Help we did; and our relentless execution both before and during Alabama launched our domestic disaster response program, which has catapulted Team Rubicon into the upper tier of US-based emergency response organizations.

Three years later, with a budget twenty times as large, we still find ourselves relying on relentless execution. During the response to Typhoon Haiyan, we needed to find a way to move a very large team of medics, more than a hundred, and a mountain of supplies over to the Philippines in an efficient way. A crazy idea popped into our heads—let's charter a jumbo jet.

We had no idea where to start. Who the hell do you call to rent an entire 767? Regardless, our team set out to figure it out. A few hours later I was on a call with a foundation, looking to secure the financing to pay for such an audacious plan. While on the call, Nicole slapped a piece of scrap paper against the window of my office. I HAVE A PLANE, it read. I relayed the information to the woman on the phone, who said that the foundation she represented would wire us the funds necessary to cover the costs.

We did it! Immediately we began activating the medics and booking their flights to get to Los Angeles to assemble, get equipped, and receive their briefings. Over the course of the next thirty-six hours the plane we had chartered was being prepared, the flight crew was being notified, and the necessary paperwork needed to fly a 767 across the Pacific

Ocean and into a foreign country was being completed and submitted. Then we hit a snag. The airline was demanding full payment, and the foundation, which had been notified late in the evening of the necessary funds transfer, was having difficulty getting their bank to wire the funds. On our end, our cash balance wouldn't cover the full cost, and we couldn't liquidate money out of our investment portfolio quickly enough to get it to the airline. For twenty-four hours I danced a dance with the airline and the broker, trying to work a deal. Finally, with a huge team of medics assembling and expecting to get on a plane in twelve hours to head to Manila, I had to pull the plug.

Mission failure, right? Wrong. I walked out into the Emergency Operations Center and briefed the team on what had happened. Before I was even finished explaining the situation, staffers and volunteers sprung into action—whether picking up the phones to halt shipments of supplies or logging onto websites to search for commercial air options. We were determined that we *would* push that team of medics to Manila, and indeed we did. Thanks to our relentless execution—our refusal to take no for an answer—we got them on the ground twenty-four hours later.

What is the key to relentless execution? And what is the difference between those individuals and companies that have it, and those that do not?

The key to relentless execution, quite simply, is the consistent and conscious choice of success over failure. It is living your personal life and leading your professional life in a way that acknowledges that when the stakes are high, the only thing that moves the needle from failure to success is the right attitude.

It means preparing yourself—mentally, physically, spiritually—for those crucial moments when everything is on the line. It starts with challenging yourself physically, constantly setting goals and pushing your body toward achieving them. It continues with the development of your mind, and the pursuit of expanding your depth of knowledge across a breadth of subjects. It is having the emotional support of friends and family, those that stand beside and behind you, listening to and loving you despite your faults.

Yet even the best-prepared leader can't consistently succeed through relentless execution without a team; a team that has diligently been selected and prepared for the task at hand. A team that has come together and set their individual egos aside and aligned themselves toward a common goal. Who trust one another resolutely and understand that their individual roles are subject to the needs of the team and the moment. A team that has adopted a culture of success.

Relentless execution also demands transparency. Those who have it all on the line deserve to know what that line looks like. They need to look to their leader and see someone who won't hide the brutal facts, but will instead share the reality of the collective situation. Blind followership is dangerous; relentless execution demands accountability, both up and down.

Relentless execution needs a target: a mission for the collective will of the team to rally around. Leaders must find and prioritize those targets, directing efforts to the centers of gravity that have the ability to cripple the obstacle standing in the way. In order to do this the team must know what they're facing; they must be disciplined in their effort to create an intelligence picture that will inform their decision making. They must overcome the urge to ignore the information they're confronted with—being foolhardy never got anyone anywhere.

Relentless execution demands bold and decisive action; yet, before taking that action, the team must look one another in the eye, literally or figuratively, and understand the collective risks they face. Relentless execution requires that no one be tethered to the fear of failure—and fear of failure is rooted in an inability to accept, not just know, the risks involved. In order to be willing to attack the hijackers, you have to think as if the plane has already crashed.

Relentless execution means understanding that waiting for 100 percent of the plan to develop is the strategy of quitters. Asking for 100 percent of the solution is asking for a roadmap to victory, but anyone who has taken on high-stakes endeavors knows there is no such roadmap. If you're not willing to take action with a less than perfect plan, then you're likely unwilling to do what it takes to succeed when your plan inevitably goes wrong. Relentless execution is rooted in flexibility, in the willingness to improvise, adapt, and overcome anything that gets in the way of success.

I didn't invent any of these principles. I didn't develop or refine them while lecturing at a business school or military academy. I discovered these principles through experience, by living my life; many of them I had to stumble across the hard way numerous times before they solidified. Ultimately, I discovered them because I was leading; because I had seen and seized opportunities to step up and Take Command and try to make a difference, and I've had incredible people help me along the way.

In the Introduction of this book I wrote that I don't consider myself a great leader, and that is certainly true. Greatness is a myth that supposes there is a destination, an end to your journey of growth as a person or organization. As a leader I am on an endless journey, a journey with an unknown destination. Along the way I am learning lessons from the situations I face, the people I lead, and the failures I encounter. The principles in this book represent a roadmap of the road I've already walked; and I only hope that they will continue to light the path ahead as I continue on my journey.

By reading and living by these principles, I have no doubt that you can embark on a similar journey, one that will allow you to choose success over failure in the high-stakes situations you face in your own life—be they personal or professional. All you have to remember is to prepare, analyze, decide, and act. It is simple, really. When life presents you with situations seemingly beyond your control, don't flinch. Instead, relentlessly execute. Take Command.

ACKNOWLEDGMENTS

I want to thank my beautiful wife for allowing me to pursue my passion, and for being a steadfast rock during turbulent times. I love you more than you know.

And my family, who over the years have molded me into the man I am today. In particular, I want to thank my father. Since leaving high school, I've come to understand just how rare it has become to have a strong father figure in one's life; and I am left eternally grateful to have had mine. He has been a source of advice throughout my life. He demanded early on that my actions match my words. Every time we parted ways he shook my hand and stated, "Use good judgment," no matter where I was off to. His final words to me as I stepped off for Afghanistan, "Bring your honor home intact," guided me every day. To this day he is a sounding board for every hard decision I make at Team Rubicon, and we're a better organization because of it.

To Sergeants Kyle Rosenberger and Shawn Beidler, two of the finest Marines I ever met. You taught me how to follow while teaching me how to lead, and you ensured that I came home from two tough tours with my honor clean. And to the handful of men from the Second Battalion, Seventh Marines, that I had the honor and privilege of leading in combat; you each made me a better man.

To William McNulty, my good friend, partner, and chief contrarian. Team Rubicon would not exist if not for his efforts, contributions, and willingness to make me better. From the beginning he has had a vision, and through great personal sacrifice he has made it a reality. And to Anthony Allman, our partner at POS REP, who defines the entrepreneurial spirit that is capable of overcoming adversity and hardship. Many of the lessons in this book we learned together. #AllIn

To Matt Pelak, JC McGreehan, Nicole Green, Ford Sypher, Josh Webster, Zach Smith, Joanne Dennis, Mike Lee, Shane Valverde, Ryan Mills, Cal Verdin, and Andrew Stevens for believing in the vision of Team Rubicon when it was nothing but a sparkle in our respective eyes. And to the hundreds of others—too many to name—who have picked up the banner and continued to carry it forward with their leadership and blood, sweat, and tears. You have created a lasting institution that means everything to thousands.

Finally, to my agent, Sydelle, and my editor on this book, Talia; who irresponsibly believed that a foul-mouthed, partially literate Marine could write a book about leadership worth reading. History will be your judge!

ABOUT THE AUTHOR

Jake Wood is CEO and cofounder of Team Rubicon and a former Marine sniper with tours in Iraq and Afghanistan. He has been profiled by *Forbes, People,* and CNN, has been named a 2012 CNN Hero, and was awarded the 2011 *GQ* Better Men Better World Award. www.Jake-Wood.com.

Team Rubicon (TR) is a disaster relief organization that unites military veterans with first responders to rapidly deploy emergency response teams to areas hit by natural disasters. TR is widely recognized for its organizational efficiency and ability to be one of the first to reach the most devastated, remote, and needy areas. Since 2010, Team Rubicon has been instrumental in more than 50 missions, ranging from South Sudan and Haiti to Joplin, Missouri, and Hurricane Sandy. www.TeamRubiconUSA.org.

Team Rubicon, which you read about throughout this book, is a 501c3 nonprofit organization that is able to accomplish its mission of deploying military veterans for disaster relief because of the generosity of its supporters. If you would like to support Team Rubicon's efforts please visit the website at www.teamrubiconusa.org and consider making a tax-deductible donation.

TO LEARN MORE ABOUT LEADING IN HIGH-STAKES SITUATIONS, BOOK JAKE WOOD TO SPEAK AT YOUR COMPANY OR ORGANIZATION

Jake Wood shares more leadership lessons and stories from the military and the disaster zone in his frequent speeches and keynotes to corporations, nonprofits, universities, and veterans' organizations. Popular topics include:

How to Lead and Succeed When It Matters Most

We live in uncertain times and are all searching for firm ground. We all want to be the one who remains steady even as others lose their footing. In today's fast-paced world of business, no matter what we do at our job or what level of leadership we have reached, there will come a time where we will be confronted with a situation in which the stakes are high, the risks considerable, and the options less than ideal. It might be a key business decision, a mistake we made in the past, or an upset customer wanting quick answers to tough questions. Whatever the issue is, being equipped to face uncertainty is always the preferred course of action.

Drawing from his experience in the military and with Team Rubicon, Jake Wood provides the framework to thrive in high-stakes situations. This talk outlines the how, when, and why of resolute, lead-from-the-front leadership, offering a set of principles that one can draw upon to Take Command in any high-stakes business situation.

Service Above Self

Jake has discovered one principle that has changed his life—and can change yours—PUT OTHERS FIRST. In our "me"-driven world, it is often difficult to remember to look outside ourselves to discover the incredible impact we can have on the world. In this inspiring story of a young man's move from self-centered yearnings to a life of service and personal sacrifice, Jake will share with the audience the deep impact of placing service about self. Jake's soul searching will have a profound effect on each attendee.

To book Jake to speak at your conference or organization, please contact the Bright Sight Group at info@brightsightgroup.com or (609) 942-3060.